ISBN 978-1-333-73880-8
PIBN 10541451

1 MONTH OF
FREE
READING

at

www.ForgottenBooks.com

By purchasing this book you are eligible for one month membership to ForgottenBooks.com, giving you unlimited access to our entire collection of over 700,000 titles via our web site and mobile apps.

To claim your free month visit:

www.forgottenbooks.com/free541451

English
Français
Deutsche
Italiano
Español
Português

www.forgottenbooks.com

Mythology Photography **Fiction**
Fishing Christianity **Art** Cooking
Essays Buddhism Freemasonry
Medicine **Biology** Music **Ancient**
Egypt Evolution Carpentry Physics
Dance Geology **Mathematics** Fitness
Shakespeare **Folklore** Yoga Marketing
Confidence Immortality Biographies
Poetry **Psychology** Witchcraft
Electronics Chemistry History **Law**
Accounting **Philosophy** Anthropology
Alchemy Drama Quantum Mechanics
Atheism Sexual Health **Ancient History**
Entrepreneurship Languages Sport
Paleontology Needlework Islam
Metaphysics Investment Archaeology
Parenting Statistics Criminology
Motivational

THE YOUNG SCIENTIST,

A Practical Journal for Amateurs.

ISSUED MONTHLY.   Price 50 Cents per year.

It is characteristic of young Americans that they want to be DOING something. They are not content with merely *knowing* how things are done, or even with *seeing* them done; they want to do them themselves. In other words, they want to experiment. Hence the wonderful demand that has sprung up for small tool chests, turning lathes, scroll saws, wood carving tools, telegraphs, model steam engines, microscopes and all kinds of apparatus. In nine cases out of ten, however, the young workman finds it difficult to learn how to use his tools or apparatus after he has got them. It is true that we have a large number of very excellent text-books, but these are not just the thing. What is wanted is a living teacher. Where a living teacher cannot be found, the next best thing is a live journal, and this we propose to furnish. And in attempting this it is not our intention to confine ourselves to mere practical directions. In these days of knowledge and scientific culture, the " Why " becomes as necessary as the " How." The object of the YOUNG SCIENTIST is to give clear and easily followed directions for performing chemical, mechanical and other operations, as well as simple and accurate explanations of the principles involved in the various mechanical and chemical processes which we shall undertake to describe.

The scope and character of the journal will be better understood from an inspection of a few numbers, or from the list of contents found on a subsequent page, than from any labored description. There are, however, three features to which we would call special attention:

CORRESPONDENCE.—In this department we intend to place our readers in communication with each other, and in this way we hope to secure for every one just such aid as may be required for any special work on hand.

EXCHANGES.—An exchange column, like that which has been such a marked success in the *Journal of Microscopy*, will be opened in the YOUNG SCIENTIST. Yearly subscribers who may wish to *exchange* tools, apparatus, books, or the products of their skill, can state what they have to offer and what they want, *without charge.* Buying and selling must, of course, be carried on in the advertising columns.

ILLUSTRATIONS.—The journal will make no claims to the character of a " picture book," but wherever engravings are needed to make the descriptions clear they will be furnished. Some of the engravings which have already appeared in our pages are as fine as anything to be found in the most expensive journals.

Special Notice.

As our journal is too small and too low-priced to claim the attention of news dealers, we are compelled to rely almost wholly upon subscriptions sent directly to this office. As many persons would no doubt like to examine a few numbers before becoming regular subscribers, we will send four current numbers as a trial trip for

FIFTEEN CENTS.

CLUBS.

Where three or more subscribe together for the journal, we offer the following liberal terms:

3 copies for.. $1.25
5   "   " 2.00

WHAT PEOPLE SAY OF US.

In a letter to the Editor, Oliver Wendel Holmes, the genial "Autocr of the Breakfast Table," says: "I am much pleased with the You Scientist. It makes me want to be a boy again."

"It is a little publication, calculated to call out and educate all t latent ingenuity and thirst for knowledge which the youthful mind po sesses, and we hope it will win its way into every household in the land."—[Scientific Press.

"We have never seen a periodical, designed for youth, which ca nearer to our ideal of what such a journal should be."—[Canadian Pha maceutical Journal.

"The Young Scientist is one of the choicest publications for juveni minds in this country. Every page treats on subjects of importance young and old, portrayed in a clearly comprehensive manner, which once interests the young idea in its careful perusal."—[Lapeer Clarion.

"It seems to fill the bill."—[Newport Daily News.

"It is pleasing to note that its youthful subscribers will not be misl by clap-trap advertisements or advertisements of patent medicines, whi will not be received at any price. The Young Scientist is doing go work in setting its face against this class of humbugs."—[Manufacturi and Trade Review.

"The work is a copiously illustrated monthly, and is full of practic hints that will instruct and amuse the young folks."—[Industrial Scho Advocate.

"A small but elegant and very instructive monthly."—[Pittsbu Chronicle.

"Contains the best possible reading for the young of both sexes." [Ottawa Journal.

"We can safely recommend this magazine as one of the very be publications for the young folks."—[The Independent, Fenton, Mich.

"This journal occupies a new field, and is needed to put the minds our youth on the right track to secure a correct understanding of t nature of things."—[Wayland Press.

"It is ably edited by John Phin, who will make a large place in t heart of the rising generation, if he persists in his venture. We hope l success in the field will be equal to the article furnished—first best." [Sunset Chimes.

"The articles are written in a popular, readable style, and profuse illustrated."—Akron City Times.

"The Young Scientist is excellent in conception, and well designed amuse and instruct young people."—[Chicago Evening Journal.

"The Young Scientist is a handsome monthly magazine, each numb containing about 16 pages, handsomely illustrated. It will supply place which has been heretofore unoccupied. The copy before us com fully up to the promise of the prospectus."—[The Times, Iroquois, Mic

"It is a journal which should be in the hands of both young and ol and is a great benefit to the young scientist as well as the advanced pr fessor. It is a thousand times more valuable than the dime novel seri so much read by boys. Parents would do well to have it in their hou holds."—[The Iron Home.

"This publication is a new launch, and it is very gratifying to witne

T

ISS

It i
They
seein
to ex
ches
engi
ever.
para
exce
ing 1
live
our i
of kr
"Ho
dire
simp
mec.

Th
spec
pag e
whic

Cc
mur
just

E
succ
Year
proc
with
tisi

I
ture
the
our

A
deal
to t
bef
tria

W
libe

A
A

THE

AMATEUR'S HANDBOOK

OF

PRACTICAL INFORMATION

FOR THE WORKSHOP AND THE LABORATORY,

CONTAINING CLEAR AND FULL DIRECTIONS FOR

Bronzing, Lacquering, Polishing Metal, Staining and Polishing Wood, Soldering, Brazing, Working Steel, Tempering Tools, Case‑hardening, Cutting and Working Glass, Varnishing, Silvering, Gilding, Preparing Skins, Waterproofing, Making Alloys, Fusible Metals, Freezing Mixtures, Polishing Powders, Signal Lights, Harmless Colored Fires for Tableaux, Catgut, Cements, Glues, &c., &c.

SECOND EDITION.—GREATLY ENLARGED.

PRICE 15 CENTS.

NEW YORK:

THE INDUSTRIAL PUBLICATION CO.

1879.

☞ *A Copy of this book will be sent to any Address post-paid on receipt of 15 one-cent stamps. Industrial Pub. Co., 176 Broadway, N. Y.*

THE G

PREFACE TO FIRST EDITION.

It is a fact well known to the editors of scientific and technical journals, that there are a series of questions to which answers are continually desired by new subscribers, no matter how often these questions may have been previously discussed. To give a reply to every one, in the columns of the journal, would be an injustice to other readers; to reply to each by letter would be an endless task, and to ignore them entirely would be inadmissible. Fortunately the majority of these questions may be fully and thoroughly answered once for all in a few pages of type, and this is the end and aim of the present work, which has been published at a price which places it within the reach of all.

The utmost care has been taken to give none but trustworthy directions and recipes. Most persons who have occasion to consult an ordinary book of recipes must be painfully aware of the fact that accuracy seems to be the last quality sought for by the compilers and indeed by most of those who contribute recipes to our technical journals. With them complexity is in more favor than efficiency, and we therefore see long lists of ingredients strung out one after the other, most of them being useless and some being even injurious. All this we have tried to avoid, and we feel confident that the amateur and those whose skill and experience is not very great will find here an efficient guide.

New York, October, 1878.

PREFACE TO SECOND EDITION.

That this little book supplied a real want has been very well shown by the rapidity with which the first edition, though a large one, has been sold off. In this edition we have given a good deal of new matter and it is hoped that in its extended form it will be still more acceptable to those who desire information of the kind which it contains.

Editor Young Scientist.

New York, February, 1879.

CONTENTS.

CONTENTS.

CONTENTS.

Alloys.

Alloy for filling holes in Iron.—Lead, 9 ; antimony, 2 ; bismuth, 1. This alloy expands in cooling, so that when a hole is filled with the melted alloy, the plug is not loose when it is cold.

Aluminium Silver.—Copper, 70 ; nickel, 23 ; aluminum, 7. Has a beautiful color and takes a high polish.

Amalgam for Silvering the insides of Globes, etc.—1. Lead, 2oz ; tin, 2oz ; bismuth, 2oz ; mercury, 4oz. Melt the first three and add the mercury. The glass being well cleaned, is carefully warmed and the melted amalgam is poured in and the vessel turned round until all parts are coated. At a certain temperature this amalgam adheres readily to glass.

2. Bismuth, 8 ; lead, 5 ; tin, 3 ; mercury, 8. Use as directed for No. 1.

Amalgam for Electrical Machines.—1. Tin, 1oz ; zinc, 1oz ; mercury, 2oz.

2. Bœttger's. Zinc, 2oz ; mercury, 1oz. At a certain temperature (easily found by experiment) it powders readily and should be kept in a tightly corked bottle. Said to be very good.

Copper Amalgam.—Dissolve 3oz. sulphate of copper in water and add 1oz. sulphuric acid Hang clean iron scraps in the solution until the copper has fallen down in fine powder. Wash this powder, and for each ounce of powder take

7oz. of mercury. To incorporate the mercury and copper, first moisten the latter with protonitrate of mercury and then add the mercury and rub up in a mortar. When thoroughly mixed wash off all acid. This amalgam is easily moulded, adheres readily to glass, takes a fine polish and becomes quite hard in a short time.

Babbitt's Anti-Attrition Metal for lining Boxes.—First melt four pounds of copper, and, when melted, add, by degrees, twelve pounds best quality Banca tin ; then add eight pounds regulus of antimony, and then twelve pounds more of tin, while the composition is in a melted state. After the copper is melted, and four or five pounds of tin have been added, the heat should be lowered to a dull red heat, in order to prevent oxidation ; then add the remainder of the metal. In melting the composition it is better to keep a small quantity of powdered charcoal in the pot, on the surface of the metal.

The above composition is made in the first place and is called hardening ; for lining work take one pound of the hardening and melt with two pounds Banca tin, which produces the very best lining metal. So that the proportions for lining metal is four pounds copper, eight regulus of antimony and ninety-six pounds tin.

The object in first preparing the hardening is economy, for when the whole is melted together there is a great waste of metal, as the hardening is melted at a much less degree of heat than the copper and antimony separately.

Fusible Alloys.—1. Bismuth, 8 ; lead, 5 ; tin, 3. . Melts with the heat of boiling water.

2. Lead, 3 ; tin, 2 ; bismuth, 5. Melts at 197 degrees, Fahrenheit.

3. Bismuth, 15 ; lead, 8 ; tin, 4 ; cadmium, 3. Melts between 150 and 160 deg. Fahr.

Pewter.—Tin, 4 ; lead, 1.

Type Metal.—Lead, 44 ; antimony, 8 ; tin, 1.

Brazing and Soldering.

The term *soldering* is generally applied when fusible alloys of lead and tin are employed. When hard metals, such as copper, brass or silver are used, the term *brazing* (derived from brass) is more appropriate.

In uniting tin, copper, brass, etc., with any of the soft solders, a copper soldering-iron is generally used. This tool and the manner of using it are too well known to need description. In many cases, however, the work may be done more neatly without the soldering-iron, by filing or turning the joints so that they fit closely, moistening them with soldering fluid, placing a piece of smooth tin-foil between them, tying them together with binding wire and heating the whole in a lamp or fire till the tin-foil melts. We have often joined pieces of brass in this way so that the joints were quite invisible. Indeed, with good soft solder almost all work may be done over a lamp without the use of a soldering-iron.

Advantage may be taken of the varying degrees of fusibility of solders to make several joints in the same piece of work. Thus, if the first joint has been made with fine tinner's solder, there would be no danger of melting it in making a joint near it with bismuth solder, composed of lead, 4, tin, 4, and bismuth, 1, and the melting point of both is far enough removed from that of a solder composed of lead, 2, tin, 1, and bismuth, 2, to be in no danger of fusion during the use of the latter.

Soft solders do not make malleable joints. To join brass, copper or iron so as to have the joint very strong and malleable, hard solder must be used. For this purpose equal parts of silver and brass will be found excellent, though for iron, copper, or very infusible brass nothing is better than silver coin rolled out thin, which may be done by any silversmith or dentist. This makes decidedly the toughest of all joints, and as a little silver goes a long way, it is not very expensive.

For most hard solders borax is the best flux. It dissolves any oxides which may exist on the surface of the metal and protects the latter from the further action of the air, so that the solder is enabled to come into actual contact with the surfaces which are to be joined. For soft solders the best flux is a soldering fluid which may be prepared by saturating equal parts of water and hydrochloric acid (spirit of salt) with zinc. The addition of a little sal ammoniac is said to improve it. In using ordinary tinner's solder, resin is the best and cheapest flux. It possesses this important advantage over chloride of zinc, that it does not induce subsequent corrosion of the article to which it is applied. When chlorides have been applied to any thing that is liable to rust, it is necessary to see that they are thoroughly washed off and the articles carefully dried.

More minute directions may be found in the *Young Scientist*, vol. I, page 56.

Bronzing.

Two distinct processes have had this name applied to them. The first consists in staining brass work a dark brown or bronze color and lacquering it; the second consists in partially corroding the brass so as to give it that greenish hue which is peculiar to ancient brass work. The first is generally applied to instruments and apparatus, the second to articles of ornament.

Bronze for Brass Instruments.—1. The cheapest and simplest is undoubtedly a light coat of plumbago or black lead. After brushing the article with plumbago place it on a clear fire till it is made too hot to be touched. Apply a plate brush as soon as it ceases to be hot enough to burn the brush. A few strokes of the brush will produce a dark brown polish approaching black, but entirely distinct from the well known appearance of black lead. Lacquer with any desired tint.

2. Plate powder or rouge may be used instead of plumbago and gives very beautiful effects.

3. Make the articles bright, then dip in aqua fortis, which must be thoroughly rinsed off with clean water. Then make the following mixture : Hydrochloric acid, 6 lbs.; sulphate of iron, ½ lb.; white arsenic, ½ lb. Be careful to get all the ingredients pure. Let the articles lie in the mixture till black, take out and dry in hot sawdust, polish with black lead and lacquer with green lacquer.

Antique Bronze.—Dissolve 1oz. sal-ammoniac, 3oz. cream tartar and 6oz. common salt in 1 pint of hot water; add 2oz. nitrate of copper dissolved in ½ pint of water ; mix well and, by means of a brush, apply it repeatedly to the article, which should be placed in a damp situation.

Browning Gun Barrels.

To obtain a handsomely browned barrel we must not only use a first rate recipe but we must apply a good deal of skill and no small amount of hard work. When barrels are imperfectly browned the fault lies more frequently in defective work than in the use of a poor recipe.

The following are the directions given in the United States Ordnance Manual, and it is to be presumed that these are the directions that are followed in the government armories.

Materials for Browning Mixture.—Spirits of wine, 1½oz.; tincture of steel, 1½oz.; corrosive sublimate, 1½oz.; sweet spirits of nitre, 1½oz.; blue vitriol, 1oz.; nitric acid, ¾oz. To be mixed and dissolved in one quart of warm water, the mixture to be kept in glass bottles and not in earthen jugs.

Previous to commencing the operation of browning it is necessary that the barrel or other part should be made quite bright with emery or a fine smooth file (but not burnished), after which it must be carefully cleaned from all greasiness ; a small quantity of powdered lime rubbed well over every part of the barrel, is the best for this purpose. Plugs of wood are then to be put into the muzzle of the barrel and into the vent, and the mixture applied to every part with a clean sponge or rag. The barrel is then to be exposed to the air for twenty-four hours, after which time it is to be well rubbed over with a steel *scratch-card* or *scratch-brush*, until the rust is entirely removed ; the mixture may then be applied again, as before, and in a few hours the barrel will be sufficiently corroded for the operation of scratch-brushing to be repeated. The same process of scratching off the rust and applying the mixture is to be repeated twice or three times a day for four or five days, by which time the barrel will be of a very dark brown color.

When the barrel is sufficiently brown and the rust has been carefully removed from every part, about a quart of boiling water should be poured over every part of the barrel in order that the action of the acid mixture upon the barrel may be destroyed and the rust thereby prevented from rising again.

The barrel, when cold, should afterwards be rubbed over with linseed oil or sperm oil. It is particularly directed that the steel scratch-card or scratch-brush be used in the place of a hard hair-brush, otherwise the browning will not be durable nor have a good appearance.

Varnish for Browned Iron.—Shellac, 1oz.; dragon's blood, $\frac{3}{16}$ of an oz.; alcohol, 1 quart.

Very complete directions for browning barrels may be found in a little book called "Shooting on the Wing," which may be obtained from the publishers of this volume.

Case Hardening.

1. Where it is desired that the articles should be hard-

ened to a considerable depth : char a quantity of bones just enough (*and no more*) to enable you to powder them with a hammer. Lay a layer of this bone dust over the bottom of an iron tray or box, which may be easily made by bending heavy sheet iron into form. Lay the articles to be hardened on the bone dust, taking care that they do not touch each other. Cover with bone dust and fill up the tray with spent dust, charcoal or sand. Expose to a bright cherry red heat for half an hour or an hour and then turn the entire contents of the tray into a vessel of cold water. We have seen beautiful results obtained by this process when carried out in a common kitchen stove.

2. Where mere superficial hardening is required, heat the article to be hardened to a bright cherry red ; sprinkle it liberally with powdered prussiate of potash. The salt will fuse, and if the piece of iron is small and gets cooled, heat it again and plunge into cold water.

Cements.

Aquarium Cement.—Litharge, fine, white, dry sand and plaster of Paris, each 1 gill; finely pulverized resin, ⅓ gill. Mix thoroughly and make into a paste with boiled linseed oil to which dryer has been added. Beat it well and let it stand four or five hours before using it. After it has stood for 15 hours, however, it loses its strength. Glass cemented into its frame with this cement is good for either salt or fresh water. It has been used at the Zoölogical Gardens, London, with great success. It might be useful for constructing tanks for other purposes or for stopping leaks.

Armenian Cement.—The jewellers of Turkey, who are mostly Armenians, have a singular method of ornamenting watch-cases, etc., with diamonds and other precious stones by simply gluing or cementing them on. The stone is set in gold or silver, and the lower part of the metal made flat or to correspond with that part to which it is to be fixed. It is then warmed gently and the glue applied, which is so very strong that the parts thus cemented never separate. This glue, which will firmly unite bits of glass and even polished steel, and may of course be applied to a vast variety of useful purposes, is thus made : Dissolve five or six bits of gum mastic, each the size of a large pea, in as much alcohol as will suffice to render it liquid ; in another vessel dissolve as much isinglass, previously a little softened in water, (though none of the water must be used,) in good brandy or rum, as will make a two ounce phial of very strong glue, adding two small bits of gum galbanum, or ammoniacum, which must be rubbed or ground until they are dissolved. Then mix the whole with a sufficient heat, keep the glue in a phial closely stopped, and when it is to be used set the phial in boiling water. To avoid the cracking of the phial by exposure to such sudden heat, use a thin green glass phial, and hold it in the steam for a few seconds before immersing it in the hot water.

Buckland's Cement for Labels.—Finely powdered white sugar, 1oz.; finely powdered starch, 3oz.; finely powdered gum arabic, 4oz. Rub well together in a dry mortar; then little by little add cold water until it is of the thickness of melted glue ; put in a wide mouthed bottle and cork closely. The powder, thoroughly ground and mixed, may be kept for any length of time in a wide mouthed bottle, and when wanted a little may be mixed with water with a stiff brush.

Cement for Glass, Earthenware, etc.—Dilute white of egg with its bulk of water and beat up thoroughly. Mix to the consistence of thin paste with powdered quicklime. Must be used immediately.

Cement for Kerosene Lamps.—The cement commonly used is plaster of Paris, which is porous and quickly penetrated by the kerosene. Another cement which has not this defect is made with three parts of resin, one of caustic soda and five of water. This composition is mixed with half its weight of plaster of Paris. It sets firmly in about three-quarters of an hour. It is said to be of great adhesive power, not permeable to kerosene, a low conductor of heat and but superficially attacked by hot water.

Cement for attaching Leather to Metal.—Wash the metal with hot gelatine ; steep the leather in an infusion of nut galls (hot) and bring the two together.

Cement for Leather Belting.—One who has tried everything says that after an experience of fifteen years he has found nothing to equal the following : Common glue and isinglass, equal parts, soaked for 10 hours in just enough water to cover them. Bring gradually to a boiling heat and add pure tannin until the whole becomes ropy or appears like the white of eggs. Buff off the surfaces to be joined, apply this cement warm, and clamp firmly.

Cement for attaching Metal to Glass.—Copal varnish, 15 ; drying oil, 5 ; turpentine, 3. Melt in a water bath and add 10 parts slacked lime.

Cementing Labels to Metal.—For attaching labels to tin and other bright metallic surfaces, first rub the surface with a mixture of muriatic acid and alcohol ; then apply the label with a very thin coating of the paste and it will adhere almost as well as on glass.

Cheese Cement for mending China, etc.—Take skim milk cheese, cut it in slices and boil it in water. Wash it in cold water and knead it in warm water several times. Place it warm on a levigating stone and knead it with quicklime. It will join marble, stone or earthenware so that the joining is scarcely to be discovered.

Chinese Cement (Schio-liao).—To three parts of fresh beaten blood are added four parts of slaked lime and a little alum; a thin, pasty mass is produced, which can be used immediately. Objects which are to be made specially waterproof are painted by the Chinese twice, or at the most three times. Dr. Scherzer saw in Pekin a wooden box which had travelled the tedious road via Siberia to St. Petersburg and back, which was found to be perfectly sound and waterproof. Even baskets made of straw became, by the use of this cement, perfectly serviceable in the transportation of oil. Pasteboard treated therewith receives the appearance and strength of wood. Most of the wooden public buildings of China are painted with schio-liao, which gives them an unpleasant reddish appearance, but adds to their durability. This cement was tried in the Austrian department of Agriculture, and by the "Vienna Association of Industry," and in both cases the statements of Dr. Scherzer were found to be strictly accurate.

Chinese Cement.—Shellac dissolved in alcohol. Used for joining wood, earthenware, glass, etc.

Faraday's Cap Cement.—Electrical Cement.—Resin, 5oz.; beeswax, 1oz.; red ochre or Venetian red in powder, 1oz. Dry the earth thoroughly on a stove at a temperature above 212 deg. Melt the wax and resin together and stir in the powder by degrees. Stir until cold lest the earthy matter settle to the bottom. Used for fastening brass work to glass tubes, flasks, etc.

Glue is undoubtedly the most important cement used in the arts. Good glue is hard, clear (not necessarily light-colored, however,) and free from bad taste and smell. Glue which is easily dissolved in *cold* water is not strong. Good glue merely swells in cold water and must be heated to the boiling point before it will dissolve thoroughly. Great care must be taken not to burn it and, therefore, it should always be prepared in a water bath.

Iron Cement for closing the Joints of Iron Pipes.—Take

of iron borings coarse powdered, 5 pounds; powdered sal-ammoniac, 2oz.; sulphur, 1oz., and water sufficient to moisten it. This composition hardens rapidly; but if time can be allowed it sets more firmly without the sulphur. It must be used as soon as mixed and rammed tightly into the joints.

Cast Iron Cement.—Take sal-ammoniac, 2oz.; sublimed sulphur, 1oz.; cast-iron filings or fine turnings, 1 lb. Mix in a mortar and keep the powder dry. When it is to be used, mix it with twenty times its weight of clean iron turnings or filings, and grind the whole in a mortar; then wet it with water until it becomes of convenient consistence, when it is to be applied to the joint. After a time it becomes as hard and strong as any part of the metal.

Japanese Cement.—Paste made of fine rice flour.

Liquid Glue.—1. Dissolve 8oz. glue in $\frac{1}{2}$ pint of water and add slowly $2\frac{1}{2}$oz. strong nitric acid.

2. Dissolve glue in strong vinegar.

Mouth Glue or Portable Glue.—Good glue, 1lb.; isinglass, 4oz. Soften in water, boil and add $\frac{1}{4}$lb. fine brown sugar. Boil till pretty thick and pour into moulds.

Mucilage for Labels.—1. Macerate 5 parts of good glue in 18 parts of water. Boil and add 9 parts rock candy and 3 parts gum arabic.

2. Mix dextrine with water and add a drop or two of glycerine.

3. A mixture of 1 part of *dry* chloride of calcium, or 2 parts of the same salt in the *crystallized* form, and 36 parts of gum arabic, dissolved in water to a proper consistency, forms a mucilage which holds well, does not crack by drying and yet does not attract sufficient moisture from the air to become wet in damp weather.

Paris Cement for mending Shells and other specimens.—Gum arabic, 5; sugar candy, 2. White lead.

Paste.—1. The best paste is made of good flour, well boiled. Resin, etc., do more harm than good.

2. An excellent white paste may be made by dissolving 2½oz. gum arabic in 2 quarts hot water and thickening with wheat flour. To this is added a solution of alum and sugar of lead ; the mixture is heated and stirred till about to boil, when it is allowed to cool.

3. Four parts, by weight, of glue are allowed to soften in 15 parts of cold water for some hours, and then moderately heated till the solution becomes quite clear. 65 parts of boiling water are now added with stirring. In another vessel 30 parts of starch paste are stirred up with 20 parts of cold water, so that a thin milky fluid is obtained without lumps. Into this the boiling glue solution is poured, with constant stirring, and the whole is kept at the boiling temperature. After cooling 10 drops of carbolic acid are added to the paste. This paste is of extraordinary adhesive power and may be used for leather, paper, or cardboard with great success. It must be preserved in closed bottles to prevent evaporation of the water, and will, in this way, keep good for years.

4. Rice flour makes an excellent paste for fine paper work.

Sorel's Cement.—Mix commercial zinc white with ⅓ its bulk of fine sand, adding a solution of chloride of zinc of 1.26 specific gravity, and rub the whole thoroughly together in a mortar. The mixture must be applied at once, as it hardens very quickly.

Transparent Cement for glass.—Fine Canada balsam.

Turner's Cement.—Melt 1lb. of resin in a pan over the fire and, when melted, add a ¼ of a lb. of pitch. While these are boiling add brick dust until, by dropping a little on a cold stone, you think it hard enough. In winter it may be necessary to add a little tallow. By means of this cement a piece of wood may be fastened to the chuck, which will hold when cool; and when the work is finished it may be removed by a smart stroke with the tool. Any traces of the cement may be removed from the work by means of benzine.

Wollaston's White Cement for large objects.—Beeswax, 1oz.; resin, 4oz.; powdered plaster of Paris, 5oz. Melt together. To use, warm the edges of the specimen and use the cement warm.

Desilvering.

To Dissolve the Silver off old Plated Goods.—Mix 1oz. of finely powdered saltpetre with 10oz. sulphuric acid and steep the goods in this mixture. If diluted with water it acts on copper and other metals, but if very strong it dissolves the silver only, and may be used to dissolve silver off plated goods without affecting the other metals.

Etching.

Etching Liquid for Steel.—Mix 1oz. sulphate of copper, $\frac{1}{4}$oz. of alum and $\frac{1}{2}$ a tea-spoonful of salt reduced to powder, with 1 gill of vinegar and 20 drops of nitric acid. This liquid may be used either for eating deeply into the metal or for imparting a beautiful frosted appearance to the surface, according to the time it is allowed to act. Cover the parts you wish to protect from its influence with beeswax, tallow, or some similar substance.

Etching on Glass.—Fancy work, ornamental figures lettering and monograms are most easily and neatly cut into glass by the sand blast process, a simple apparatus for which will be found described in the *Young Scientist*. Lines and figures on tubes, jars, etc., may be deeply etched by smearing the surface of the glass with beeswax, drawing the lines with a steel point and exposing the glass to the fumes of hydrofluoric acid. This acid is obtained by putting powdered fluor spar into a tray made of sheet lead and pouring sulphuric acid on it, after which the tray is slightly warmed.

Gilding.

Gilding on Leather, Cloth, etc.—1. Articles of this kind may be gilded by first smearing them with diluted white of egg and then stamping the pattern (letters or any other device) with a hot metallic stamp. The superfluous gold is removed by means of a tuft of cotton. To gild wood, etc., first make the surface quite smooth, then coat with gold size, and when the latter has dried so as to be *tacky*, apply gold leaf. When well dried burnish with some smooth tool, preferably a bit of agate.

2. Ornamental lines of gilding may be painted on wood and other articles by means of a fine camel hair brush, using shell gold, which may be had at the artists' supply stores.

Gilding Metals.—Polished steel may be beautifully gilded by means of the ethereal solution of gold. Dissolve pure gold in aqua regia, evaporate gently to dryness, so as to drive off the superfluous acid, re-dissolve in water and add three times its bulk of sulphuric ether. Allow to stand for twenty-four hours in a stoppered bottle and the ethereal solution of gold will float at top. Polished steel dipped in this is at once beautifully gilded, and by tracing patterns on the surface of the metal with any kind of varnish, beautiful devices in plain metal and gilt will be produced. For other metals the electro process is the best.

Glass Working.

Glass is usually brought into shape by being moulded or blown. Simple and complete directions for blowing small articles may be found in the *Young Scientist*, vol. i, p. 37.

There are a few other operations, however, which are con-stantly needed by the amateur and which we will describe.

Cutting Glass.—For cutting flat glass, such as window-panes, and for cutting rounds or ovals out of flat glass, the diamond is the best tool; and, if the operator has no dia-mond it will always pay to carry the job to a glazier rather than waste time and make a poor job by other and inferior means. When, however, it is required to cut off a very lit-tle from a circle or oval, the diamond is not available, ex-cept in very skilful hands. In this case a pair of pliers soft-ened by heating, or very dull scissors is the best tool, and. the cutting is best performed under water. A little practice will enable the operator to shape a small round or oval with great rapidity, ease and precision. When bottles or flasks are to be cut, the diamond is still the best tool in skilful hands; but ordinary operators will succeed best with pas-tilles, or a red hot poker with a pointed end. We prefer the latter, as being the most easily obtained and the most effi-cient; and we have never found any difficulty in cutting off broken flasks so as to make dishes, or to carry a cut spirally round a long bottle so as to cut it into the form of a cork-screw. And, by the way, when so cut, glass exhibits consid-erable elasticity, and the spiral may be elongated like a ringlet. The process is very simple. The line of the cut should be marked by chalk or by pasting a thin strip of paper alongside of it; then make a file mark to commence the cut; apply the hot iron and a crack will start; and this crack will follow the iron wherever we choose to lead it. In this way jars are easily made out of old bottles, and broken vessels of different kinds may be cut up into new forms. Flat glass may also be cut into the most intricate and elegant forms. The red hot iron is far superior to strings wet with turpentine, friction, etc.

Drilling Glass.—For drilling holes in glass, a common

steel drill, well made and well tempered, is the best tool. The steel should be forged at a low temperature, so as to be sure not to burn it, and then tempered as hard as possible in a bath of salt water that has been well boiled. Such a drill will go through glass very rapidly if kept well moistened with turpentine in which some camphor has been dissolved. Dilute sulphuric acid is equally good, if not better. It is stated, that at Berlin, glass castings for pump-barrels, etc., are drilled, planed and bored, like iron ones, and in the same lathes and machines, by the aid of sulphuric acid. A little practice with these different plans will enable the operator to cut and work glass as easily as brass or iron.

Turning Glass in the Lathe.—Black diamonds are now so easily procured that they are the best tools for turning, planing or boring glass where much work is to be done. With a good diamond a skilful worker can turn a lens out of a piece of flat glass in a few seconds, so that it will be very near the right shape.

Glass Stoppers.—To remove glass stoppers when tightly fixed, it has been recommended to apply a cloth wet in hot water. This is an inconvenient and frequently unsuccessful method. The great object is to expand the neck of the bottle so as to loosen it on the stopper. If, however, the latter be heated and expanded equally with the former the desired effect is not produced; and this is often the case in applying hot water. By holding the neck of the bottle about half an inch above the flame of a lamp or candle, for a few seconds, we have never failed in the most obstinate cases. The hands should be wrapped in a towel and great care should be taken not to let the flame touch the glass, as this might cause it to crack. The bottle should be kept rapidly turning, during the operation, so as to bring all parts of the neck equally under the influence of the heat, when it will be rapidly expanded and the stopper may be withdrawn by a *steady* pull and twist. Sometimes it is necessary to tap the stopper lightly with a piece of wood ; the jar is very apt to loosen the stopper. To twist the stopper, make, in a piece of wood, an oblong hole into which the stopper will just fit.

Hardening and Annealing Copper, Brass, etc.

Copper, brass, German silver and similar metals are hardened by hammering, rolling or wire-drawing and are softened by being heated red hot and plunged in water. Copper, by being alloyed with tin, may be made so hard that cutting instruments may be made of it. This is the old process of hardening copper, which is so often claimed to be one of the lost arts.

Inks.

Black Ink.—1. In 1 gallon of water boil 1lb. bruised Aleppo galls for two hours and strain when cold. Dissolve $5\frac{1}{2}$oz. sulphate of iron and 5oz. gum arabic in as little water as is necessary and mix the two liquids with constant stirring. Keep in a tall bottle, allow it to settle for some days and it will be ready for use.

2. It is said that the juice of elderberries to which sulphate of iron has been added, makes a good ink. The best formula is said to be $12\frac{1}{2}$ pints juice and $\frac{1}{2}$oz. each sulphate of iron and crude pyroligneous acid.

Runge's Black Ink.—Digest $\frac{1}{4}$lb. logwood in chips for 12 hours in 3 pints boiling water. Simmer down gently to 1 quart, filter and add 20 grains yellow chromate of potassa.

Blue Ink.—Take 6 drachms pure Prussian blue and 1 drachm oxalic acid. Grind in a mortar with a little water until they form a perfectly smooth paste. Dissolve a sufficient quantity of this paste in water to give the proper tint.

Carmine Ink.—Dissolve 12 grains pure carmine in 3 oz. water of ammonia and add 18 grains powdered gum arabic

Red Ink.—Boil ½lb. of Brazil wood, ¼oz. of gum, ½oz. of sugar and ½oz. of alum in a sufficient quantity of vinegar.

Marking Ink for Linen.—Dissolve ¼oz. nitrate of silver in 1oz. water and add strong liquid ammonia until the precipitate which is at first formed is redissolved. Add 1½ drachm gum mucilage and enough coloring matter to render the writing clearly visible. The writing is made black by passing a hot iron over it. Keep in the dark.

Gold Ink.—Grind gold leaf with honey in a mortar until it is reduced to a fine powder. Wash out the honey with hot water and add mucilage of gum arabic. A cheap article may be made by using yellow bronze powder.

Silver Ink.—Prepared in the same way as gold ink, using silver leaf or silver bronze powder.

Sympathetic Ink or *Secret Ink.*—1. Write with thin solution of starch and let the correspondent wash with solution of iodine.

2. Write with milk, onion juice or lemon juice, and let the correspondent expose to heat.

3. Write with solution of tartar emetic and wash with any alkaline sulphuret. Letters may be written on postal cards with these inks, and will remain invisible until washed with the appropriate solution or exposed to heat. To prevent the letters from being seen by close scrutiny the solutions should be very dilute, and to distract the attention of those not in the secret, write some unimportant matter, in lines far apart, and between them write the private matter in secret or sympathetic ink.

Lacquer.

Lacquer is so called because it usually contains gum *lac,* either shellac or seed lac. Seed lac is the original form of the gum or resin; after being purified it is moulded into thin sheets, like shell, and hence is called *shellac.* Shellac is frequently bleached so as to become quite white, in which state it forms a colorless solution. Bleached shellac is never as strong as the gum in its natural condition, and unless it be fresh it neither dissolves well in alcohol nor does it preserve any metal to which it may be applied.

There are many recipes for good lacquer, but the success of the operator depends quite as much upon skill as upon the particular recipe employed. The metal must be cleaned perfectly from grease and dirt, and in lacquering new work it is always best to lacquer as soon after polishing as possible. Old lacquer may be removed with a strong lye of potash or soda, after which the work should be well washed in water, dried in fine beech or box-wood sawdust and polished with whiting, applied with a soft brush. The condition of the work, as to cleanliness and polish, is perhaps the most important point in lacquering.

The metal should be heated and the lacquer applied evenly with a soft camel hair brush. A temperature of about that of boiling water will be found right.

Lacquer is colored either red with dragon's blood or yellow with turmeric or gamboge. The following are a few favorite recipes.

Deep Gold Lacquer.—Alcohol, ½ pint; dragon's blood, 1 drachm; seed lac, 1½oz.; turmeric, ¼oz. Shake up well for a week, at intervals of, say, a couple of hours; then allow to settle, and decant the clear lacquer; and if at all dirty filter through a tuft of cotton wool. This lacquer may be diluted with a simple solution of shellac in alcohol and will then give a paler tint.

Bright Gold Lacquer.—1. Turmeric, 1oz.; saffron ¼oz.; Spanish anatto, ¼oz.; alcohol, 1 pint. Digest at a gentle heat for several days; strain through coarse linen; put the tincture in a bottle and add 3oz. good seed lac coarsely pow dered. Let it stand for several days, shaking occasionally Allow to settle and use the clear liquid.

2. Take 1oz. anatto and 8oz. alcohol. Mix in a bottle by themselves. Also mix separately 1oz. gamboge and 8oz. alcohol. With these mixtures color seed lac varnish to suit yourself. If it be too red add gamboge; if too yellow add anatto; if the color be too deep, add spirit. In this manner you mav color brass of any desired tint.

Pale Gold Lacquer.—Best pale shellac (picked pieces). 8oz.; sandarac, 2oz.; turmeric, 8oz.; anatto, 2oz.; dragon's blood, ¼oz.; alcohol, 1 gallon. Mix, shake frequently till the gums are dissolved and the color extracted from the coloring matters and then allow to settle.

Lacquer used by A. Ross.—4oz. shellac and ¼oz. gamboge are dissolved by agitation, without heat, in 24oz. pure pyro-acetic ether. The solution is allowed to stand until the gummy matters, not taken up by the spirit, subside. The clear liquor is then decanted, and when required for use is mixed with 8 times its quantity of alcohol. In this case the pyro-acetic ether is employed for dissolving the shellac in order to prevent any but the purely resinous portions being taken up, which is almost certain to occur with ordinary alcohol; but if the lacquer were made entirely with pyro-acetic ether, the latter would evaporate too rapidly to allow time for the lacquer to be equally applied.

Lubricators.

Fine Lubricating Oil.—1. Put fine olive oil in a bottle with scrapings of lead and expose it to the sun for a few weeks. Pour off the clear oil for use.

2. Freeze fine olive oil, strain out the liquid portion and preserve for use.

Booth's Axle Grease.—Dissolve ½lb. washing soda in 1 gallon water and add 3lbs. tallow and 6lbs. palm oil. Heat to 210 deg. Fahr., and keep constantly stirring until cooled to 60 or 70 deg.

Anti-Attrition.—Mix 4lbs. tallow or soap with 1lb. finely ground plumbago. The best lubricator for wood working on wood. Excellent for wooden screws where great power is required.

Polishing Metals.

Metals are polished either by burnishing or buffing. The process of burnishing consists in rubbing down all the minute roughnesses by means of a highly polished steel or agate tool—none of the metal being removed. Buffing is performed by rubbing the metal with soft leather, which has been charged with very fine polishing powder. The rubbing is sometimes done by hand but more frequently the buff is made into a wheel which revolves rapidly in a lathe and the work is held against it. The best polishing powder is crocus or rouge, which may be purchased of any dealer in tools or may be made by exposing very clean and pure crystals of sulphate of iron to heat. Those portions which are least calcined, and are of a scarlet color, are suitable for soft metals like gold or silver; those which have become red, purple or bluish purple are fit for brass or steel. The hardest part will be found at the bottom of the crucible.

Polishing Wood.

Turned articles must be brought to a fine smooth surface with the finest sand-paper and the direction of the motion should be occasionally reversed so that the fibres which are laid down by rubbing one way may be raised up and cut off. To apply the polish, which is merely a solution of shellac in alcohol, take three or four thicknesses of linen rag and place a few drops of polish in the centre; lay over this a single thickness of linen rag and a drop or two of raw linseed oil over the polish. The rubber is then applied with light friction over the entire surface of the work while revolving in the lathe, never allowing the hand or mandrel to remain still for an instant, so as to spread the varnish as evenly as possible, especially at the commencement, and paying particular attention to the internal angles, so as to prevent either deficiency or excess of varnish at those parts. The oil, in some degree, retards the evaporation of the spirit from the varnish and allows time for the process; it also presents a smooth surface and lessens the friction against the tender gum. When the varnish appears dry, a second, third and even further quantities are applied in the same manner, working, of course, more particularly upon those parts at all slighted in the earlier steps.

Flat surfaces are polished in a similar manner. The wood must first be *filled,* as it is called, and for this nothing is better than whiting colored so as to resemble the wood and kept dry. Rub the wood with linseed oil and then sprinkle it with whiting. Rub the latter well in, wipe it off carefully and give time to dry. This is far superior to size.

The polisher, however, generally consists of a wad of list rolled spirally, tied with twine and covered with a few thicknesses of linen rag. Apply a little varnish to the middle of the rubber and then enclose the latter in a soft linen rag folded twice. Moisten the face of the linen with a little raw linseed oil applied to the middle of it by means of the finger. Pass the rubber quickly and lightly over the surface of the work in small circular strokes until the varnish becomes nearly dry; charge the rubber with varnish again and repeat the rubbing till three coats are laid' on, when a little oil may be applied to the rubber and two more coats given it. Proceed in this way until the varnish has acquired some thickness; then wet the inside of the linen cloth, before applying the varnish, with alcohol and rub quickly, lightly and uniformly the whole surface. Lastly wet the linen cloth with a little oil and alcohol, without varnish, and rub as before till dry. Each coat is to be rubbed until the rag appears dry, and too much varnish must not be put on the rag at one time. Be also very particular to have the rags clean, as the polish depends in a great degree upon keeping everything free from dust and dirt.

Silvering.

Leather, cloth, wood and similar materials are silvered by processes similar to those used for gilding, (page 20), silver leaf being substituted for gold leaf. Metals may be silvered either by brazing a thin sheet of silver to the surface or by electro-plating. Frequently, however, it is desired to lightly silver a metal surface, such as brass or copper, so as to make any figures engraved thereon appear more distinct. Clock faces, dials and the scales of thermometers and barometers are cases in point, and if the surface be well lacquered with white lacquer after being silvered, such a coating is very durable. Silvering fluids or powders containing mercury should never be used unless the articles are to be afterwards exposed to a red heat so as to drive off the mercury. A silvering fluid which is very commonly sold to housekeepers under the name of *Novargent* or *Plate Renovator*, consists merely of nitrate of mercury or quicksilver. When rubbed on a copper cent or a brass stair-rod it gives it at once a bright silvery surface, but the brightness soon fades and the article, if brass, becomes black and dirty, while if it should be a piece of plated ware it will be ruined. Stair-rods and similar articles, if well silvered with powder No. 1 and then lacquered with good lacquer, will present a white silvery appearance for a long time. Plated goods should be recoated by the electro-plating process.

Silvering Powder.—1. Nitrate of silver, 30 grains; common salt, 30 grains; cream tartar, 200 grains. Mix. Moisten with water and rub on the article with wash leather. Gives a white silvery appearance to brass, copper, etc.

2. *Novargent.*—Add common salt to a solution of nitrate of silver until the silver has all been precipitated. Wash the white precipitate or chloride of silver and add a strong solution of hyposulphite of soda until the white chloride is dissolved. Mix the resulting clear liquid with pipe-clay which has been finely powdered and thoroughly washed.

3. *Silvering Amalgam.*—A coating of silver, heavier than can be obtained by the above, may be given by the following process: Precipitate silver from its solution in nitric acid by means of copper. Take of this powder ½oz.; common salt, 2oz.; sal ammoniac, 2oz.; and corrosive sublimate, 1 drachm. Make into a paste with water. Having carefully cleaned the copper surface that is to be plated, boil it in a solution of tartar and alum, rub it with the above paste, heat red hot and then polish.

Skins—Tanning and Curing.

Curing Fur Skins.—The following are the directions given in the Trapper's Guide, by Newhouse, an experienced trapper and hunter. 1. As soon as possible after the animal is dead, attend to the skinning and curing. The slightest taint of putrefaction loosens the fur and destroys the value of the skin. 2. Scrape off all superfluous flesh and fat, but be careful not to go so deep as to cut the fibre of the skin. 3. Never dry a skin by the fire or in the sun, but in a cool, shady place, sheltered from rain. If you use a barn door for a stretcher, nail the skin on the *inside* of the door. 4. Never use "preparations" of any kind in curing skins, nor even wash them in water, but simply stretch and dry them as they are taken from the animal. In drying skins it is important that they should be stretched tight like a drum-head.

To prepare Sheep Skins for Mats.—Make a strong lather with hot water and let it stand till cold; wash the fresh skin in it, carefully squeezing out all the dirt from the wool ; wash it in cold water till all the soap is taken out. Dissolve a pound each of salt and alum in 2 gallons of hot water, and put the skin into a tub sufficient to cover it ; let it soak for 12 hours and hang it over a pole to drain. When well drained, stretch it carefully on a board to dry and stretch several times while drying. Before it is quite dry sprinkle on the flesh side 1oz. each of finely· pulverized alum and saltpetre, rubbing them in well. Try if the wool be firm on the skin ; if not, let it remain a day or two, then rub again with alum ; fold the flesh sides together and hang in the shade for 2 or 3 days, turning them over each day till quite dry. Scrape the flesh side with a blunt knife and rub it with pumice or rotten stone. Very beautiful mittens can be made of lambs' skins prepared in this way.

Skins of Rabbits, Cats and small Animals.—Lay the skin on a smooth board, the fur side undermost, and fasten it down with tinned tacks. Wash it over first with a solution of salt ; then dissolve 2½oz. of alum in 1 pint of warm water, and with a sponge dipped in this solution, moisten the surface all over ; repeat this every now and then for 3 days. When the skin is quite dry take out the tacks, and rolling it loosely the long way, the hair side in, draw it quickly backwards and forwards through a large smooth ring until it is quite soft, and then roll it in the contrary way of the skin and repeat the operation. Skins prepared in this way are useful in many experiments and they make good gloves and chest protectors.

Staining Wood.

This process may be used either for improving the natural color of wood or for changing it so completely as to give it the appearance of an entirely different kind of timber. Thus a light mahogany may be greatly improved by being made darker, and there are many other kinds of timber that are greatly improved by a slight change in their color. The following notes will be of use in the latter direction:

A solution of asphaltum in spirits of turpentine, makes a good brown stain for coarse oaken work, which is only intended to be varnished with boiled oil.

When discolored ebony has been sponged once or twice with a strong decoction of gall-nuts, to which a quantity of iron filings or rust has been added, its natural blackness becomes more intense.

The naturally pale ground and obscure grain of Honduras mahogany is often well brought out by its being coated first with spirits of hartshorn and then with oil which has been tinged with madder or venetian red.

Grayish maple may be whitened by carefully coating it with a solution of oxalic acid to which a few drops of nitric acid have been added.

Half a gallon of water in which ½lb. of oak bark and the same quantity of walnut shells or peels have been thoroughly boiled, makes an excellent improver of inferior rose-wood; it is also far before any other of its kind for bringing out walnut.

Raw oil mixed with a little spirits of turpentine, is universally allowed to be the most efficacious improver of the greater number of materials. Beautiful artificial graining may be imparted to various specimens of timber by means of a camel-hair pencil, with raw oil alone, that is, certain portions may be coated two or three times very tastefully, so as to resemble the rich varying veins which constitute the fibril figures; while the common plain parts, which constitute the ground shades, may only be once coated with the oil, very much diluted with spirits of turpentine. The following are a few useful stains:

Mahogany.—1. Water, 1 gallon; madder, 8oz.; fustic, 4oz. Boil. Lay on with a brush while hot, and while wet streak it with black to vary the grain. This imitates Honduras mahogany.

2. Madder, 8oz.; fustic, 1oz.; logwood, 2oz.; water, 1 gallon. Boil and lay on while hot. Resembles Spanish mahogany.

3. A set of pine shelves, which were brushed two or three times with a strong boiling decoction of logwood chips and varnished with solution of shellac in alcohol, appear almost like mahogany both in color and hardness. After washing with decoction of logwood and *drying thoroughly*, they received two coats of varnish. They were then carefully sand-papered and polished and received a final coat of shellac varnish.

Imitation Ebony.—Wash any compact wood with a boiling decoction of logwood 3 or 4 times, allowing it to dry between each application. Then wash it with a solution of acetate of iron, which is made by dissolving iron filings in vinegar. This stain is very black and penetrates to a considerable depth into the wood, so that ordinary scratching or chipping does not show the original color. Some recipes direct the solutions of logwood and iron to be mixed before being applied, but this is a great mistake.

Black Walnut Stain.—1. Take asphaltum, pulverize it, place it in a jar or bottle, pou ·r it about twice its bulk of turpentine, put it in a warm ... ce and shake it from time to time. When dissolved, strain it and apply it to the wood with a cloth or stiff brush. If it should make too dark a stain thin it with turpentine. This will dry in a few hours. If it is desired to bring out the grain still more apply a mixture of boiled oil and turpentine; this is better than oil alone. Put no oil with the asphaltum mixture or it will dry very slowly. When the oil is dry the wood can be polished with the following: Shellac varnish, of the usual consistency, 2 parts; boiled oil, 1 part. Shake it well before using. Apply it to the wood by putting a few drops on a cloth and rubbing briskly on the wood for a few moments. This polish works well on old varnished furniture.

2. The appearance of walnut may be given to white woods by painting or sponging them with a concentrated warm solution of permanganate of potassa. The effect is different on different kinds of timber, some becoming stained very rapidly, others requiring more time for the result. The permanganate is decomposed by the woody fibre ; brown peroxide of manganese is precipitated, and the potash is af-terwards removed by washing with water. The wood, when dry, may be varnished.

Brown Stain.—Paint over the wood with a solution made by boiling 1 part of catechu (cutch or gambier) with 30 parts of water and a little soda. This must be allowed to dry in the air, and then the wood is to be painted over with another solution made of 1 part of bichromate of potash and 30 parts of water. By a little difference in the mode of treatment and by varying the strength of the solutions, various shades of color may be given with these materials, which will be permanent and tend to preserve the wood.

Steel—Working and Tempering.

Most amateurs will find themselves, at times, compelled to forge and temper their own tools, such as drills, cold chisels, etc. The following hints will be of service.

Forging Steel.—Beware of over-heating the piece to be forged and also be careful that the fire is free from sulphur. Small drills are easily heated in the flame of a lamp or candle ; a Bunsen burner will heat sufficiently quite a good sized tool. Charcoal makes the best fire for large tools. If you are compelled to use common coal let the fire burn until most of the sulphur has been driven off. Do not hammer with heavy blows after the steel has cooled. By tapping it lightly, however, until it becomes black, the closeness of the grain is increased.

To Restore burnt Cast Steel.—Heat it to a bright cherry red and quench it in water. Do this a few times and then forge it carefully and it will be as good as ever. The various recipes for mixtures for restoring burnt steel are worthless.

Hardening and Tempering Steel.—Heat the steel to a bright cherry red and plunge it in water that has been thoroughly boiled and then allowed to cool. It will then be "as hard as fire and water will make it," and too hard for anything except hardened bearings or tools for cutting and drilling glass and very hard metals. To make it stand work without breaking it must be *tempered.* To do this, polish the surface on a grindstone or with emery paper, so that any change in the color of the metal may be easily seen. Then heat the tool until the cutting edge shows the proper color, as given below. Large drills and cold chisels are hardened and tempered at one operation, the cutting edge being cooled and hardened while the upper part is left hot. When taken from the water the heat from the shank passes towards the cutting edge and brings it to the right degree of softness. Small drills have to be tempered in the flame of a lamp. A spirit lamp is best, and the neatest plan is to heat the drill a short distance from the point and allow the heat to flow towards the cutting edge. As soon as the right color is seen on the edge, the entire tool is plunged in water and cooled. In this way the shank is kept soft and the tool is not so apt to snap off.

The following are the degrees of heat (Fahrenheit) and corresponding colors to which tools for different purposes should be brought :

TEMPERATURE.	COLOR.	TEMPER.
430°	Very faint yellow.	Very hard; suitable for hammer faces, drills for stone, etc.
450°	Pale straw color.	
470°	Full yellow.	Hard and inelastic; suitable for shears, scissors, turning tools for hard metal, etc.
490°	Brown.	
510°	Brown with purple spots.	Suitable for tools for cutting wood and soft metals, such as plane irons, knives, etc.
538°	Purple.	
550°	Dark blue.	For tools requiring strong cutting edges without extreme hardness; as cold chisels, axes, cutlery, etc.
560°	Full blue.	
600°	Grayish blue verging on black.	Spring temper; saws, swords.

Varnishes.

It is in general more economical to buy varnishes than to make them on the small scale. Occasionally, however, our readers may find themselves in a situation where a simple recipe for a good varnish will prove valuable. We append a few recipes which are easily followed.

White Spirit Varnish.—Rectified spirit, 1 gallon; gum sandarach, 2½lbs. Put these ingredients into a tin bottle, warm gently and shake till dissolved. Then add a pint of pale turpentine varnish.

Shellac Varnish.—Dissolve good shellac or seed lac in alcohol, making the varnish of any consistence desired. NOTE.—Shellac gives a pale cinnamon colored varnish. Varnish made with seed lac is deeper colored and redder. If colorless varnish is desired use bleached shellac, an article which is to be had at most drug stores.

Turpentine Varnish.—Clear pale resin, 5lbs.; turpentine, 7lbs. Dissolve in any convenient vessel.

Varnish for Violins and similar articles.—Sandarach, 6oz.; mastic, 3oz.; turpentine varnish, ½ pint; alcohol, 1 gallon. Keep in a tight tin can in a warm place until the gums are dissolved.

White, Hard Varnish for Wood or Metal.—Mastic, 2oz.: sandarach, 8oz.; elemi, 1oz.; Strasbourgh or Scio turpentine, 4oz.; alcohol, 1 quart.

White Varnish for Paper, Wood or Linen.—Sandarach, 8oz.; mastic, 2oz.; Canada balsam, 4oz.; alcohol, 1 quart.

Mastic.—Mastic, 6oz.; turpentine, 1 quart. Tough, hard, brilliant and colorless. Excellent for common woodwork.

Map Varnish.—Clear Canada balsam, 4oz ; turpentine, 8oz. Warm gently and shake until dissolved. Maps, drawings, etc., which are to be varnished with this solution, should be first brushed over with a solution of isinglass and allowed to dry thoroughly.

Varnish for Bright Iron-work.—Dissolve 3lbs. of resin in 10 pints boiled linseed oil and add 2lbs. of turpentine.

Black Varnish for Iron-work.—Fuse 40oz. of asphaltum and add ½ a gallon of boiled linseed oil, 6oz. red lead, 6oz. litharge, and 4oz. sulphate of zinc, dried and powdered. Boil for 2 hours and mix in 8oz. fused dark amber gum and a pint of hot linseed oil and boil again for 2 hours more. When the mass has thickened withdraw the heat and thin. down with a gallon of turpentine.

Waterproofing.

Porous goods are made waterproof according to two very distinct systems. According to the first the articles are made absolutely impervious to water and air by having their pores filled up with some oily or gummy substance, which becomes stiff and impenetrable. Caoutchouc, paints, oils, melted wax, etc., are of this kind. The other system consists in making the fabric *repellent* to water while it remains quite porous and freely admits the passage of air. Goods so prepared will resist any ordinary rain, and we have seen a very porous fabric stretched over the mouth of a vessel and resist the passage of water one or two inches deep. The following recipes have been tried and found good. Most of those found in the recipe books are worthless.

To render Leather Water-proof.—1. Melt together 2oz. of Burgundy pitch, 2oz. of soft wax, 2oz. of turpentine, and 1 pint of raw linseed oil. Lay on with a brush while warm.

2. Melt 3oz. lard and add 1oz. powdered resm. This mixture remains soft at ordinary temperatures, and is an excellent application for leather.

Water-proof Canvas for Covering Carts, etc.—$9\frac{1}{2}$ gallons linseed oil, 1lb. litharge, 1lb. umber, boiled together for 24 hours. May be colored with any paint. Lay on with a brush.

To Make Sailcloth Impervious to Water, and yet Pliant and Durable.—Grind 6lbs. English ochre with boiled oil, and add 1lb. of black paint, which mixture forms an indifferent black. An ounce of yellow soap, dissolved by heat in half a pint of water, is mixed while hot with the paint. This composition is laid upon dry canvas as stiff as can conveniently be done with the brush. Two days after a second coat of ochre and black paint (without any soap) is laid on, and, allowing this coat time to dry, the canvas is finished with a coat of any desired color. After three days it does not stick together when folded up. This is the formula used in the British navy yards, and it has given excellent results. We have seen a portable boat made of canvas prepared in this way and stretched on a skeleton frame.

The following recipes are intended to be applied to woven fabrics, which they leave quite pervious to air but capable of resisting water.

1. Apply a strong solution of soap to the wrong side of the cloth, and when dry wash the other side with a solution of alum.

2. Take the material successively through baths of sulphate of alumina, of soap and of water; then dry and smother or calender. For the alumina bath, use the ordinary neutral sulphate of alumina of commerce (concentrated alum cake), dissolving 1 part in 10 of water, which is easily done without the application of heat. The soap is best prepared in this manner: Boil 1 part of light resin, 1 part of soda crystals, and 10 of water, till the resin is dissolved; salt the soap out by the addition of $\frac{1}{3}$ part of common salt; dissolve this soap with an equal amount of good palm-oil soap in 30 parts of water. The soap bath should be kept hot while the goods are passing through it. It is best to have three vats alongside of each other, and by a special arrangement to keep the goods down in the baths. Special care should be taken to have the fabric thoroughly soaked in the alumina bath.

3. Drs. Hager and Jacobsen remark that during the last few years very good and cheap waterproof goods of this description have been manufactured in Berlin, which they believe is effected by steeping them first in a bath of sulphate of alumina and of copper, and then into one of water-glass and resin soap.

Freezing Mixtures.

The temperatures here given are Fahrenheit. When ice or snow are not to be had and it is desired to cool any solid, liquid or gas, a good freezing mixture is the simplest method of accomplishing the object. The following mixtures are the most convenient and efficient :

1. Nitrate of ammonia, carbonate of soda and water, equal parts by weight. The thermometer sinks 57°

2. Phosphate of soda, 9 parts ; nitrate of ammonia, 6 parts ; diluted nitric acid, (acid 1 part, water 2 parts,) 4 parts. Reduces the temperature 71° or from 50° to —21.°

3. Sal ammoniac, 5 parts ; nitrate of potash, 5 parts ; sulphate of soda, 8 parts; water, 16 parts. Reduces the temperature 46° or from 70° to 24°. This is one of the cheapest, most readily procured, and most convenient of mixtures.

Freezing mixtures are often used when it is required to produce a greater degree of cold than can be obtained by the mere application of ice. When ice is at hand, as it generally is in this country, the following should be used :

1. Finely pounded ice, 2 parts; salt 1 part. This mixture reduces the temperature to 5°.

2. Finely pounded ice, 2 parts ; crystallized chloride of calcium, 3 parts. Reduces the temperature from 32° to —40°.

3. Finely pounded ice, 7 parts; diluted nitric acid, 4 parts. Reduces the temperature from 32° to —30°.

In every case the materials should be kept as cool as possible. Thus the ice should be pounded in a cooled mortar with a cooled pestle, and the mixture should be made in vessels previously cooled. By attention to these particulars it is easy to freeze mercury at any time by means of these simple and easily practiced methods, though, of course, the modern laboratory is provided with agencies of far greater cooling power.

Paper.

There are so many purposes to which paper is applied that a small volume might be filled with a description of them. The following are those which will probably prove most useful to the amateur:

Tracing Paper.—Tracing paper may be purchased so cheaply that it is hardly worth while to make it; and there is a very fine, tough kind now in market which may be mounted and colored almost like drawing paper. Those who desire to prepare some for themselves will find that the following directions give a good result. The inventor of the process received a medal and premium from the Society of Arts for it.

Open a quire of tough tissue paper, and brush the first sheet with a mixture of equal parts of mastic varnish and oil of turpentine. Proceed with each sheet similarly and, dry them on lines by hanging them up singly. As the process goes on, the under sheets absorb a portion of the varnish, and require less than if single sheets were brushed separately. The paper, when dry, is quite light and transparent and may readily be written on with ink.

Transfer Paper.—This is useful for copying patterns, drawings, etc. Designs for scroll saws may be copied very neatly by means of it. It is easily made by rubbing a thin but tough unglazed paper with a mixture of lard and lampblack. The copy is made by laying a sheet of the transfer or, as it is sometimes called, *manifold* paper, over a clean sheet of drawing or writing paper and over it the drawing to be copied. The lines of the drawing are then carefully traced with a fine but blunt point and the pressure along the lines transfers to the clean paper underneath a perfect copy. To keep the underside of the drawing or pattern clean, a sheet of tissue paper may be placed between it and the transfer paper.

Waxed Paper.—Paper saturated with wax, paraffin or stearin is very useful for wrapping up articles which should be kept dry and not exposed to the air. Place a sheet of stout paper on a heated iron plate, and over this place the sheets of unglazed paper—tissue paper does very well—that are to be waxed. Enclose the wax or paraffin in a piece of muslin and as it melts spread it evenly over the paper.

Polishing Powders.

The principal polishing powders are chalk or whiting, crocus or rouge, emery, oilstone powder, and putty or tutty, which latter consists chiefly of oxide of tin. Other powders, such as tripoli, bath brick, sand, etc., are rarely used for the finer kinds of work. Emery is so well known that it does not need description.

Chalk or Whiting.—Chalk is a native carbonate of lime, consisting of the remains of minute creatures known as *for-aminifera*, and when simply scraped or crushed under a hammer or runner, it is sometimes used for polishing such soft substances as bone, ivory, etc. As it contains particles of silica of varying size, it cuts freely, but is apt to scratch. To remove the gritty particles, the chalk is ground, and the finer parts separated by washing. It then becomes *whiting*, which is generally sold in lumps. Whiting has very poor cutting qualities, and it is therefore used chiefly as *plate powder* for cleaning gold, silver, glass, etc., and for absorbing grease from metals which have been polished by other means.

Prepared Chalk.—This is a manufactured article, prepared by adding a solution of carbonate of soda to a solution of chloride of calcium (both cheap salts), so long as a precipitate is thrown down. The solutions should be carefully filtered through paper before being mixed, and dust should be rigorously excluded. The white powder which falls down is carbonate of lime, or chalk, and when carefully washed and dried, it forms a most excellent polishing powder for the softer metals. The particles are almost impalpable, but seem to be crystalline, for they polish quickly and smoothly, though they seem to wear away the material so little that its form or sharpness is not injured to any perceptible degree.

Crocus or Rouge.—These articles are manufactured at Liverpool, by persons who make it their sole occupation, in the following manner ·

They take crystals of sulphate of iron, (green vitriol or copperas,) immediately from the crystallizing vessels, in the copperas works there, so as to have them as clean as possible ; and instantly put them into crucibles or cast iron pots, and expose them to heat, without suffering the smallest particle of dust to get in, which would have a tendency to scratch the articles to be polished. Those portions which are least calcined and are of a scarlet color, are fit to make rouge for polishing gold or silver, while those which are calcined, or have become red-purple or bluish-purple, form crocus fit for polishing brass or steel. Of these, the bluish-purple colored parts are the hardest, and are found nearest to the bottom of the vessels, and consequently have been exposed to the greatest degree of heat.

Mr. Andrew Ross's mode of preparing Oxide of Iron.— Dissolve crystals of sulphate of iron in water ; filter the solution to separate some particles of silex which are generally present, and sometimes are abundant ; then precipitate from this filtered solution the protoxide of iron, by the addition of a saturated solution of soda, which must also be filtered. This grey oxide is to be repeatedly washed and then dried; put it in this state into a crucible, and very gradually raise it to a dull red heat; then pour it into a clean metal or earthen dish, and while cooling it will absorb oxygen from the atmosphere, and acquire a beautiful dark red color. In this state it is fit for polishing the softer metals, as silver and gold, but will scarcely make any impression on hardened steel or glass. For these latter purposes I discovered that it is the black oxide that affected the polish, (and this gives to the red oxide a purple hue, which is used as the criterion of its cutting quality in ordinary,) therefore for polishing the harder materials the oxide must be heated to a bright red, and kept in that state until a sufficient quantity of it is converted into black oxide to give the mass a deep purple hue when exposed to the atmosphere. I have converted the whole into black oxide; but this is liable to scratch, and does not work so pleasantly as when mixed with the softer material. The powder must now be levigated with a soft wrought iron spatula, upon a soft iron slab, and afterwards washed in a very weak solution of gum arabic, as recommended by Dr. Green in his paper on Specula. The oxide prepared in this manner is almost impalpable, and free from all extraneous matter, and has the requisite quality in an eminent degree for polishing steel, glass, the softer gems, etc.

Lord Ross's Mode of preparing the Peroxide of Iron.— " I prepare the peroxide of iron by precipitation with water of ammonia from a pure dilute solution of sulphate of iron; the precipitate is washed, pressed in a screw-press till nearly dry, and exposed to a heat which in the dark appears a dull low red. The only points of importance are, that the sulphate of iron should be pure, that the water of ammonia should be decidedly in excess, and that the heat should not exceed that I have described. The color will be a bright crimson inclining to yellow. I have tried both soda and potash, pure, instead of water of ammonia, but after washing with some degree of care, a trace of the alkali still remained, and the peroxide was of an ochrey color till over-heated, and did not polish properly."

Oilstone Powder.—Fragments of oilstone, when pulver-ized, sifted and washed, are much in request by mechanicians. This abrasive is generally preferred for grinding together those fittings of mathematical instruments and machinery, which are made wholly or in part of brass or gun metal, for oilstone being softer and more pulverulent than emery, is less liable to become embedded in the metal than emery, which latter is then apt continually to grind, and ultimately damage the accuracy of the fittings of brass works. In mod-ern practice it is usual, however, as far as possible, to dis-card the grinding together of surfaces, with the view of producing accuracy of form, or precision of contact.

Oilstone powder is preferred to pumice-stone powder for polishing superior brass works, and it is also used by the watchmaker on rubbers of pewter in polishing steel.

Pumice-stone Powder.—Pumice-stone is a volcanic pro-duct, and is obtained principally from the Campo Bianco, one of the Lipari islands, which is entirely composed of this substance. It is extensively employed in various branches of the arts, and particularly in the state of powder, for polishing the various articles of cut glass; it is also extensively used in dressing leather, and in grinding and polishing the surface of metallic plates, etc.

Pumice-stone is ground or crushed under a runner, and sifted, and in this state it is used for brass and other metal works, and also for japanned, varnished and painted goods, for which latter purposes it is generally applied on woolen cloths with water.

Putty Powder is the pulverized oxide of tin, or generally of tin and lead mixed in various proportions. The process of manufacture is alike in all cases,—the metal is oxidized in an iron muffle, or a rectangular box, close on all sides, except a square hole in the front side. The retort is surrounded by fire, and kept at a red heat, so that its contents are partially ignited, and they are continually stirred to expose fresh portions to the heated air ; the process is complete when the fluid metal entirely disappears, and the upper part of the oxide then produced, sparkles somewhat like particles of incandescent charcoal. The oxide is then removed with ladles, and spread over the bottom of large iron cooling pans and allowed to cool. The lumps of oxide which are as hard as marble, are then selected from the mass and ground dry under the runner ; the putty powder is afterwards carefully sifted through lawn.

As a criterion of quality it may be said that the whitest putty powder is the purest, provided it be heavy. Some of the common kinds are brown and yellow, while others, from the intentional admixture of a little ivory black, are known as *grey putty*. The pure white putty which is used by marble workers, opticians and some others, is the smoothest and most cutting ; it should consist of the oxide of tin alone, but to lessen the difficulty of manufacture, a very little lead, (the linings of tea chests,) or else an alloy called *shruff*, (prepared in ingots by the pewterers) is added to assist the oxidation.

The putty powder of commerce of good fair quality, is made of about equal parts of tin and lead, or tin and shruff ; the common dark colored kinds are prepared of lead only, but these are much harsher to the touch, and altogether inferior.

Perhaps the most extensive use of putty powder, is in glass and marble works, but the best kind serves admirably as plate powder, and for the general purposes of polishing.

Putty Powder for fine optical purposes is prepared by Mr. A. Ross by the following method, which is the result of many experiments. Metallic tin is dissolved in nitro-muriatic acid, and precipitated from the filtered solution by liquid ammonia, both fluids being largely diluted with water. The peroxide of tin is then washed in abundance of water, collected in a cloth filter, and squeezed as dry as possible in a piece of new clean linen; the mass is now subjected to pressure in a screw-press, or between lever boards, to make it as dry as possible. When the lump thus produced has been broken in pieces and dried in the air, it is finally levigated while dry, on a plate of glass with an iron spatula, and afterwards exposed in a crucible to a *low* white heat.

Before the peroxide has been heated, or while it is in the levigated *hydrous* state, the putty powder possesses but little cutting quality, as under the microscope, the particles then appear to have no determined form, or to be *amorphous*, and on being wetted, to resume the gelatinous condition of the hydrous precipitate, so as to be useless for polishing; whereas when the powder is heated, to render it *anhydrous*, most of the particles take their natural form, that of *lamellar crystals*, and act with far more energy, (yet without scratching) than any of the ordinary polishing powders. The whole mass requires to be washed or elutriated in the usual manner after having been heated, in order to separate the coarser particles.

Mr. Ross usually adds a little crocus to the putty powder by way of coloring matter, as it is then easier to learn the quantity of powder that remains on the polishing tool, and it may be added that this is the polishing powder employed by Mr. Ross in making his improved achromatic object glasses for astronomical telescopes.

Signal and Colored Lights.

The following recipes are from the United States Ordnance Manual, and may be considered reliable. The composition for signal lights is packed in shallow vessels of
large diameter so as to expose considerable surface. Where
the burning surface is large, the light attains great intensity,
but the material burns out rapidly. In arranging the size
and shape of the case, therefore, regard must be had to the
time the light is expected to burn and the brilliancy that is
wanted. [*See caution at end of this article.*]

Bengal Light.—Antimony, 2; sulphur, 4; mealed powder,
4; nitrate of soda, 16.

Blue.—Black sulphuret of antimony, 1; sulphur, 2;
pure nitre, 6. Grind to a very fine powder and mix thoroughly. See that the nitre is perfectly dry. This composition gives a bluish white light; a deeper blue may be had
by the addition of a little finely pulverized zinc.

Red.—1. Saltpetre, 5; sulphur, 6; nitrate of strontia,
20; lampblack, 1.

2. Nitrate of strontia, 20; chlorate of potassa, 8; sulphur,
6; charcoal, 1.

White.— Saltpetre, 16; sulphur, 8; mealed powder, 4.
Grind to a very fine powder and mix well.

The following have been very highly recommended:

Crimson Fire.—Sulphide of antimony, 4; chlorate of potassa, 5; powdered roll brimstone, 13; dry nitrate of strontia, 40 parts.

A very little charcoal added to the above makes it burn
quicker.

Green Fire.—Fine charcoal, 3; sulphur, 13; chlorate of
potassa, 8; nitrate of baryta, 77·

White.—1. Nitrate of potassa (saltpetre), 24; sulphur
7; charcoal, 1.

2. Nitre, 6 ; sulphur, 2 ; yellow sulphuret of arsenic, 1. [NOTE.—This light is a very brilliant one and a very pure white, but the fumes are highly poisonous. It should be used only in the open air and the wind should blow the vapors away from the spectators—not towards them.]

3. Chlorate of potash, 10 ; nitre, 5 ; lycopodium, 3 ; charcoal 2.

4. Metallic magnesium in the form of ribbon or wire. This is the best and most easily used. · It may be purchased of most dealers in chemicals. A few inches of magnesium ribbon coiled into a spiral (like a spiral spring) and ignited by means of a spirit lamp or even by a little tuft of cotton soaked in alcohol and fired with a lucifer match, makes a light of surpassing brilliancy and power. It requires a slight knack to ignite the ribbon. Hold the end of it steadily in the *outer edge* of the flame and it will soon take fire. The light given out by a small ribbon of magnesium is clearly visible at a distance of thirty miles.

Lights for Indoor Illuminations.—Many of the above are unfit for indoor exhibitions owing to the amount of sulphurous gas given off. For tableaux in churches, schools and private houses, the best light is undoubtedly magnesium or, where it can be had, the lime light (sometimes, though erroneously, called the calcium light). Both of these lights are very powerful, and any color may be obtained by the use of pieces of differently colored glass. A very effective arrangement consists of a tin box, which may be made out of one of those cases in which crackers are imported. Procure good-sized pieces of red and blue glass, the red being a soft, warm tint, such as will add a richness to the complexions of those upon whom the light is thrown. Arrange one end of the tin box so that these glasses may be slipped over a large hole in it. The opposite end of the box should be highly polished so as to act as a reflector, and a hole should be cut in one side so as to allow of the introduction of the magnesium.

In every case the burning matter should be so shaded that it may not be seen by the audience. If the direct light from the burning body meets the eyes of the spectators the reflected light from the objects composing the tableau will have no effect.

Where arrangements for lime or magnesium lights cannot be made, the following may be used.

White.—Chlorate of potash, 12; nitre, 5; finely powdered loaf sugar, 4; lycopodium, 2.

Green.—Nitrate of baryta, shellac and chlorate of potassa, all finely powdered, equal parts by bulk.

Red.—Nitrate of strontia, shellac and chlorate of potassa, all finely powdered, equal parts by bulk.

The brilliancy of these fires will depend largely upon the thoroughness with which the materials are finely powdered and mixed. [*See caution at end of this article.*]

Braunschweizer recommends the following formula as giving excellent results, the lights being good without producing injurious fumes:

Red.—Nitrate of strontia, 9; shellac, 3; chlorate of potassa 1½.

Green.—Nitrate of baryta, 9; shellac, 3; chlorate of potassa, 1½.

Blue.—Ammoniacal sulphate of copper, 8; chlorate of potassa, 6; shellac, 1.

Ghosts, Demons, Spectres and Murderers.—To give a ghastly hue to the faces of the actors, the best light is that produced by some salt of soda, common salt being very good. We have succeeded well in this way: A piece of wire gauze such as ash-sifters are made of, and about a foot square was supported at a height of about a foot from the floor, which was protected by a sheet of iron. On the wire gauze were laid twenty-five wads of cotton waste which had been soaked in a solution of common salt, dried and dipped in alcohol just before being laid on the wire. When these were ignited we had twenty-five powerful flames all tinged with sodium and burning freely, as the air rose readily among them through the wire grating. Such a flame produces quite a powerful light and gives a death-like appearance to even the most rosy-checked girl.

The following give a strong light and produce a most ghastly effect:

1. Nitrate of soda, 10; chlorate of potash, 10; sulphide of antimony, 3; shellac, 4. The materials must be warm and dry, and as the nitrate of soda attracts moisture rapidly it must be well dried, then finely powdered as quickly as possible and kept in well-corked bottles. As this gives off a good deal of sulphurous fumes, the following may be preferred where the ventilation is not good:

2. Nitrate of soda, 10; chlorate of potassa, 15; white sugar finely powdered, 5; lycopodium, 2.

CAUTION.

In using chlorate of potassa the greatest care is necessary. It may be powdered and otherwise handled safely when alone, but when combustible matter of any kind is added to it the mixture becomes highly explosive and must be very gently handled. It must therefore be powdered *separately* and only mixed with the other ingredients *after* they have been powdered. The mixing should be done on a large sheet of paper, very gently, but very thoroughly, with a thin, broad-bladed knife.

Mixtures of chlorate of potash with sulphur, sulphurets, and especially phosphorus, are liable to explode spontaneously after a time, and should never be kept on hand. They should be made as wanted.

MISCELLANEOUS RECIPES.

To remove the Blue Color imparted to Iron and Steel by exposure to Heat.—Rub lightly with a sponge or rag dipped in diluted sulphuric, nitric, or hydrochloric acid. When the discoloration is removed, carefully wash the article, dry it by rubbing, warm it and give a coat of oil or it will rapidly rust.

Size for Improving poor Drawing Paper.—Take 1oz. of white glue, 1oz. of white soap and ½oz. of alum. Soak the glue and the soap in water until they appear like jelly; then simmer in 1 quart of water until the whole is melted. Add the alum, simmer again and filter. To be applied hot.

To fix Pencil Marks so they will not rub out.—Take well-skimmed milk and dilute with an equal bulk of water. Wash the pencil marks, (whether writing or drawing,) with this liquid, using a soft camel-hair flat brush, and avoiding all rubbing. Place upon a flat board to dry.

Cure for Burns.—A solution of bicarbonate of soda applied to burns, promptly and permanently relieves all pain. A laboratory assistant in Philadelphia having severely burned the inside of the last joint of his thumb while bending glass tubing, applied the solution of bicarbonate of soda, and not only was the pain allayed but the thumb could be at once freely used without inconvenience. Bicarbonate of soda is simply the best baking soda.

Care of Looking Glasses.—When looking glasses are exposed to the direct rays of the sun or to very strong heat from a fire the amalgam is apt to crystallize and the mirror loses its brilliancy. If a mirror is placed where the rays of the sun can strike it, it should be covered in that part of the day during which it is exposed.

The best method of cleaning looking glasses is as follows Take a newspaper, fold it small, dip it in a basin of clean cold water. When thoroughly wet squeeze it out as you do a sponge; then rub it pretty hard all over the surface of the glass, taking care that it is not so wet as to run down in streams; in fact, the paper must only be completely moistened or dampened all through. Let it rest a few minutes, then go over the glass with a piece of fresh newspaper till it looks clear and bright. The insides of windows may be cleaned in the same way; also spectacle glasses, lamp-glasses, etc. White paper that has not been printed on is better; but in the absence of that a very old newspaper, on which the ink has become thoroughly dried, should be used. Writing paper will not answer.

Laundry Gloss.—Various recipes have been given for imparting a fine gloss to linen. Gum arabic, white wax, spermaceti, etc., have all been highly recommended and are, no doubt, useful to a certain extent, but the great secret seems to lie in the quality of the iron used and the skill of the laundress. If the iron is hard, close grained and finely polished, the work will be much easier. Laundresses always have a favorite smoothing iron with which they do most of their work, and many of them have the front edge of the iron rounded so that great pressure can be brought to bear on a very small spot instead of being spread over a space the size of the whole face of the iron. If smoothing irons have become rough and rusty it will pay to send them to a grinder to have them not only ground but *buffed,* (see article on *Polishing Metals*). The greatest care should be taken not to allow them to get spotted with rust and they should never be " brightened " with coarse sand, ashes, emery, etc. If it is necessary to polish them, rub them on a board, or preferably a piece of leather charged with the finest flour of emery, obtained by washing, or better still, jeweller's rouge.

Kalsomine.—Professors of the "Art of Kalsomining" affect a great deal of mystery, but the process is very simple. It consists simply in making a whitewash with some neutral substance which is made to adhere by means of size or glue. It contains no caustic material like lime. Several substances have been used with good results. The best is zinc white. It gives the most brilliant effect but is the most expensive. The next is Paris white or sulphate of baryta. This, when pure, is nearly equal to zinc white, but unfortunately common whiting is often sold for it and more often mixed with it. It is not difficult, however, to detect common whiting either when alone or mixed with Paris white. When vinegar or better still, spirits of salt, is poured on whiting it foams or effervesces, but produces no effect on Paris white. Good whiting, however, gives very fair results and makes a far better finish than common lime.

With any one of these three substances, or a mixture of them, a good whitewash or kalsomine may be prepared as follows: Select some very clear colorless glue and soak ¼lb. in water for 12 hours. Then boil it, taking great care that it does not burn, and this is best done by setting the vessel with the glue in a pan of water over the fire. When completely dissolved add it to a large pail of hot water and into any desired quantity of this stir as much of the white material used as will make a cream. The quality of the resulting work will depend on the skill of the operator, but we may remark that it is easier to get a smooth hard finish by using three coats of thin wash than by using one coat of thick. If you have time for but one coat, however, you must give it body enough. In giving more than one coat let the last coat contain less glue than the preceding ones

To Stain Dried Grass.—There are few prettier ornaments, and none more economical and lasting, than bouquets of dried grasses mingled with the various unchangeable flowers. They have but one fault, and that is this, the want of other colors besides yellow and drab or brown. To vary their shade artificially these flowers are sometimes dyed green. This, however, is in bad taste and unnatural. The best effect is produced by blending rose and red tints together, and with a very little pale blue with the grasses and flowers as they dry naturally. The best means of dyeing dried leaves, flowers and grasses is to dip them into the alcoholic solution of the various compounds of aniline. Some of these have a beautiful rose shade; others red, blue, orange and purple. The depth of color can be regulated by diluting, if necessary, the original dyes, with alcohol, down to the shade desired. When taken out of the dye they should be exposed to the air to dry off the alcohol. They then require arranging or setting into form, as, when wet, the petals and fine filaments have a tendency to cling together. A pink saucer, as sold by most druggists, will supply enough rose dye for two ordinary bouquets. The pink saucer yields the best rose dye by washing it off with water and lemon juice. The aniline dyes yield the best violet, mauve and purple colors.

Amalgamating Zincs for Voltaic Batteries.—When the zincs are new and uncorroded, this is an easy process. Dip the zincs in dilute sulphuric acid (8 parts water and 1 of acid) and rub them with mercury. The mercury will adhere quite readily and render the entire surface brilliant and silvery. But when the zincs are old and corroded it will be found that the mercury does not adhere to some parts. In such cases wash the surface of the zinc with a solution of nitrate of mercury and it will become coated with amalgam. Once the surface is touched, it is easy to add as much mercury as may be desired by simply rubbing on the liquid metal.

The coating of mercury adds greatly to the durability of the zincs, as when so prepared the acid will not act on them except when the current is passing, and from the excellent condition of the entire surface the power of the battery is greatly increased.

Amber, to Unite Broken Pieces.—Coat with linseed oil the surfaces that are to be joined ; hold the oiled parts carefully over a charcoal fire, a few hot cinders or a gaslight, being careful to cover up all the rest of the object loosely with paper. When the oiled parts have begun to feel the heat so as to be sticky, press and clamp them together and keep them so until nearly cold. Only that part where the edges are to be united must be warmed, and even that with care lest the form or polish of the other parts should be disturbed ; the part where the joint occurs generally requires to be repolished.

Arsenical Preservative Powder.—This is dusted over moist skins and flesh, and preserves almost any animal matter from putrefaction. It is thus made : Arsenic, 4oz ; burnt alum, 4oz ; tanner's bark, 8oz ; mix and grind together to a very fine powder.

Arsenical Soap.—This is the most powerful preservative in use. It is a strong poison, but is invaluable for preserv-

ing skins of birds and beasts that are to be stuffed. It is
made thus: Powdered arsenic, 2oz ; camphor, 5oz ; white
soap, 2oz ; salt of tartar (sub-carbonate of potash), 6 drachms ;
powdered lime 2 drachms. Cut the soap in very thin slices
and heat gently with a small quantity of water, stirring all
the time with a stick. When thoroughly melted add the
salt of tartar and the lime. When these are well mixed together add the arsenic, which must be carefully incorporated
with the other ingredients. Take the mixture off the fire
and while cooling add the camphor, previously reduced to
powder by rubbing it with a little alcohol. When finished
the soap should be of the consistence of thick cream and
should be kept in a tightly stopped bottle.

Black Varnish for Cast Iron.—For those objects to
which it is applicable, one of the best black varnishes is obtained by applying boiled linseed oil to the iron, the latter
being heated to a temperature that will just char or blacken
the oil. The oil seems to enter into the pores of the iron,
and after such an application the metal resists rust and corrosive agents very perfectly.

Black Varnish for Optical Work.—The external surfaces
of brass and iron are generally blacked or bronzed with
compositions given under the head of *lacquers.* The insides
of the tubes of telescopes and microscopes should be coated
with a dead black varnish so as to absorb the light and prevent any glare. The varnish that is generally used for this
purpose consists of lampblack, made liquid by means of a
very thin solution of shellac in alcohol, but such varnish, even
when laid on warm metal, is very apt to scale off and thus
produce two serious evils—the exposure of the bright metallic surface, and the deposit of specks on the lenses. It will
therefore be found that lampblack, carefully ground in turpentine, to which about a fifth of its volume of gold size or
boiled linseed oil has been added, will adhere much more-

firmly. The metal should be warm when the varnish is applied.

Cat-gut.—This material is so valuable for many purposes that amateur mechanics will find it useful to know how to make it. The process is quite simple. Take the entrails of sheep or other animals, remembering that fat animals afford a very weak string, while those that are lean produce a much tougher article, and thoroughly clean them from all impurities, attached fat, etc. The animal should be newly killed. Wash well in clean water and soak in soft water for two days, or in winter for three days; lay them on a table or board and scrape them with a small plate of copper having a semicircular hole cut in it, the edges of which must be quite smooth and not capable of cutting. After washing put them into fresh water and there let them remain till the next day, when they are to be well scraped. Let them soak again in water for a night, and two or three hours before they are taken out add to each gallon of water 2oz. of potash. They ought now to scrape quite clean from their inner mucous coat, and will consequently be much smaller in dimensions than at first. They may now be wiped dry, slightly twisted, and passed through a hole in a piece of brass to equalize their size; as they dry they are passed every two or three hours through other holes, each smaller than the last. When dry they will be round and well polished, and after being oiled are fit for use.

Coral, Artificial.—Twigs, raisin stalks and any objects having the general outline of branched coral may be made to resemble that material by being dipped in a mixture of 4 parts resin, 3 parts beeswax and 2 parts vermilion, melted together and thoroughly mixed. The effect is very pretty, and for ornamental work such imitation coral, is very useful.

Dresses—To Render Fire Proof.—Some years ago Queen

Victoria appointed a commission to investigate this subject. It was found that there were but four salts which were applicable to light fabrics: 1, Phosphate of ammonia; 2, a mixture of phosphate of ammonia and chloride of ammonia; 3, sulphate of ammonia; 4, tungstate of soda. Of these, the best was tungstate of soda, a salt which is not by any means expensive. Sulphate of ammonia is objectionable, from the fact that it acts on the irons and moulds the fabric. The tungstate of soda is neither injurious to the texture or color, or in any degree difficult of application in the washing process. The iron passes over the material quite as smoothly as if no solution had been employed. The solution increases the stiffness of the fabric, and its protecting power against fire is perfect. This salt offers only one difficulty, viz.: the formation of a bitungstate, of little solubility, which crystallizes from the solution; but it was found that a very small percentage of phosphate of soda rendered the tungstate quite stable. The best method of applying these salts is to take one ounce of tungstate of soda and a quarter of an ounce of phosphate of soda, and dissolve them in a quart of water. The goods are moistened with this solution before being starched, and they may be afterwards ironed and finished without the least difficulty.

Articles prepared in this way are perfectly uninflammable. They may be charred by exposure to fire, but they do not burn readily unless there is some extraneous source of heat, and they can not be made to burst into flame. By the aid of this discovery, a lady dressed in the lightest muslin might walk over a row of footlights, and the only result would be that the lower part of her dress would be injured. Unless her person actually came in contact with the gas flames, she herself would suffer no injury. In country places, where tungstate of soda cannot be procured, a mixture of three parts borax, and two and a half parts sulphate of magnesia, in twenty parts of water, may be used with good effect.

Glass-paper.—Paper coated with glass is known by this name just as paper coated with fine sharp sand is called *sand-paper,* and paper coated with emery is called *emery paper.* Paper or a cheap cloth is coated with thinnish glue, dusted heavily and evenly with glass-powder of the proper fineness, and allowed to become nearly dry. The superflu ous powder is then shaken off, the sheets are pressed to make them even and afterwards thoroughly dried.

The objection to ordinary glass-paper is that it is easily injured by heat and moisture. If the glue be mixed with a little bichromate of potassa before it is applied to the cloth, and exposed for some time to strong bright sunshine while it is drying, it will become insoluble in water.

The glue may also be rendered insoluble by the process of tanning. The paper or cloth is first soaked in a solution of tannic acid and dried. The glue is then applied, the powdered glass dusted on, and over it is dusted a little tannic acid. If the glue be not very moist, it should be damped by means of an atomizer, a very cheap form of which is figured in THE YOUNG SCIENTIST, Vol. II. The sheets are then slowly dried and will be found to resist moisture very thoroughly.

Glass—To Powder.—Powdered glass is frequently used instead of paper, cloth, cotton or sand for filtering varnishes, acids, etc. It is not soluble or corrodible. Sand, if purely silicious, would be better, but such sand is difficult to get : it too often contains matters which are easily corroded or dissolved. Powdered glass when glued to paper is also used for polishing wood and other materials. It cuts rapidly and cleanly, and is better than sand for most purposes. Glass is easily pulverized after being heated red hot and plunged into cold water. It cracks in every direction, becomes hard and brittle and breaks with keenly cutting edges. After being pounded in a mortar it may be divided into powders of different degrees of fineness by being sifted through lawn sieves.

Glass—Imitation Ground.—Put a piece of putty in muslin, twist the fabric tight, and tie it into the shape of a pad; well clean the glass first, and then putty it all over. The putty will exude sufficiently through the muslin to render the stain opaque. Let it dry hard, and then varnish. If a pattern is required, cut it out in paper as a stencil; place it so as not to slip, and proceed as above, removing the stencil when finished. If there should be any objection to the existence of the clear spaces, cover with slightly opaque varnish. In this way very neat and cheap signs may be painted on glass doors.

Glass Ware—Packing.—Every one has this duty to perform occasionally, and it is well to know how it should be done. The safety of glass articles packed together in a box does not depend so much upon the quantity of packing material used, as upon the fact that no two pieces of glass come into actual contact. In packing plates, a single straw placed between two of them will prevent them from breaking each other. In packing bottles in a case, such as the collecting case of the microscopist, and the test case of the chemist, rubber rings slipped over each, will be found the best and handiest packing material. They have this great advantage that they do not give rise to dust.

Glue—Portable.—Put a pinch of shredded gelatine into a wide-mouthed bottle; put on it a very little water, and about one-fourth part of glacial acetic acid; put in a well-fitting cork. If the right quantity of water and acid be used, the gelatine will swell up into worm-like pieces, quite elastic, but at the same time, firm enough to be handled comfortably. The acid will make the preparation keep indefinitely. When required for use, take a small fragment of the swelled gelatine, and warm the end of it in the flame of a match or candle; it will immediately "run" into a fine clear glue, which can be applied at once direct to the article to be mended. The thing is done in half a minute, and is, moreover, done well, for the gelatine so treated makes the very best and finest glue that can be had. This plan might be modified by dissolving a trace of chrome alum in the water used for moistening the gelatine, in which case, no doubt, the glue would become insoluble when set. But for general purposes, there is no need for subsequent insolubility in glue.

Javelle Water.—Take 4lbs. carbonate of soda, and 1lb. chloride of lime; put the soda into a kettle, add 1 gallon of boiling water and boil for from 10 to 15 minutes; then stir in the chloride of lime, breaking down all lumps with a wooden spatula or stirrer. Pour into large glass bottles; when cold and settled it will be ready for use.

This forms a very efficient bleaching liquid, and one which it is not difficult to remove from the bleached fabric. Old and stained engravings and books, as well as linen and cotton goods that have become yellow with dirt and age, may be rendered snowy white by the application of this liquid.

Jewelry—Cleaning.—Ordinary gold jewelry may be effectnally cleansed by washing with soap and warm water, rinsing in cold water and drying in warm box-wood saw-dust. Plain, smooth surfaces may be rubbed with chamois leather charged either with rouge or prepared chalk, but the less rubbing the better.

Silver is liable to tarnish by the action of sulphur, and where there is fine chased or engraved work the extreme delicacy of the lines may be injured by much rubbing. In such cases the articles may be cleaned by washing with a solution of hyposulphite of soda. Cyanide of potassium is a more powerful cleansing agent but is very poisonous.

Painting Bright Metals.—When paint is applied to bright

metals like tin or zinc, it is very apt to peel off. This difficulty is greatly lessened if the metal be hot when the paint
is applied, but in many cases this cannot be done. In such
cases the surface of the metal should be corroded for which
purpose a solution of sulphate of copper, acidulated with
nitric acid, answers well. The metal should be washed with
the solution, allowed to stand a couple of hours and then
washed with clean water and dried.

Pillows for the Sick-Room.— Save all your scraps of
writing paper, old envelopes, old notes of no use for keeping, old backs of notes, etc. Cut them into strips about
½ inch wide and 2 inches long, and curl them well with
an old pen-knife. Make a pillow case of any materials
you have ; fill it with your curled paper mixed with a few
shreds of flannel. Stuff it quite full, sew up the end and
cover as you please. These pillows are invaluable in cases
of fever, as they keep constantly cool and allow a circula-
tion of air.

Sieves for the Laboratory.—It is often desirable to sift
powders into different degrees of fineness, and very fine
sieves are not always to be easily had. Those made of hair
and wire answer well, but the finest may be made out of the
bolting cloth used by millers.

Silvering Glass Mirrors for Optical Purposes.—This is
best effected by depositing pure silver on the glass. The
light reflected from a mirror made thus has somewhat of a
yellowish tinge, but photometric experiments show that
from 25 to 30 per cent more light is reflected than from the
old mercurial mirrors.

Where *ammonium aldehyde* can be obtained, there is no
doubt that this is the best and most economical process,
whether used on a large or a small scale. But those who·
have not had considerable experience in the laboratory cannot always prepare this compound.

The next best process is based upon the reduction of metallic silver from its ammoniacal solution by salts of tartar. After a trial of several formulæ of this kind, all of them more or less simple, as well as efficacious, the following has been found to yield the best results in the shortest time.

Silvering Solution.—In 1 ounce of distilled or pure rain water, dissolve 48 grains of crystalized nitrate of silver. Precipitate by adding strongest water of ammonia, and continue to add the ammonia drop by drop, stirring the solution with a glass rod, until the brown precipitate is nearly, but not quite, redissolved. Filter, and add distilled water to make 12 fluid drachms.

Reducing Solution.—Dissolve in 1 ounce of distilled or very clean rain water, 12 grains of potassium and sodium tartrate (Rochelle or Seignette salts). Boil, in a flask, and while boiling add 2 grains crystalized nitrate of silver dissolved in 1 drachm of water. Continue the boiling five or six minutes. Let cool, filter, and add distilled water to make 12 fluid drachms.

To Silver.—Provision must be made for supporting the glass in a perfectly horizontal position at the surface of the liquid. This is best done by cementing to the face of the mirror three nice hooks by which it may be hung from a temporary frame work—easily made out of a few sticks.

The glass to be silvered must be cleansed by immersing it in strong nitric acid, washing in liquor potassæ, and thoroughly rinsing with distilled water. If the glass has had mercurial amalgam on it, it will probably be necessary to clean the back with rouge. On having this surface perfectly, chemically clean, depends in a great measure the success of the operation.

Having arranged the contrivance for suspending the glass so that it may be at exactly the right height in the vessel that is to receive the solution, remove this vessel and pour into it enough of equal quantities of the two solutions to fill it exactly to the previously ascertained level. Stir the solutions so that they will become thoroughly mixed, and replace the glass to be silvered, taking great care that the surface to be silvered shall come in contact with the silvering fluid exactly at all points. The glass plate should be rinsed carefully before replacing, and should be put in while wet. Great care should be taken that no air bubbles remain on the surface of the solution, or between it and the surface to be silvered.

Now set the vessel in the sun for a few minutes, if the weather be warm, or by the fire, if it be cold, as a temperature of 45o to 50o C. (113o to 122o Fah.) is most conducive to the rapid deposition of a brilliant, firm and even film of silver. The fluid in the sunlight soon becomes inky black, gradually clearing as the silver is reduced, until when exhansted it is perfectly clear. The mirror should be removed before this point is reached, as a process of bleaching sets up if left after the fluid is exhausted. From 20 to 80 minutes, according to the weather, purity of chemicals, etc., is required for the entire process.

When the mirror is removed from the bath, it should be carefully rinsed with distilled water from the wash bottle, and laid on its edge on blotting paper to dry. When perfectly dry, the back should be varnished with some elastic varnish and allowed to dry. The wires and cement can now be removed from the face, and the glass cleaned with a little fledget of cotton and a minute drop of nitric acid, taking great care that the acid does not get to the edges or under the varnish. Rinse, dry and the mirror is finished.

Water-stains, To Remove from Engravings or Paper.— Fill a large vessel with pure water and dip the engraving in, waving it backward and forward until thoroughly wet

Then spread a sheet of clean white paper on a drawing board, lay the engraving on it and fasten both to the board with drawing pins. Expose it to bright sunshine, keeping it moist until the stains disappear, which will not be long. This is simply a modification of the old system of bleaching linen.

Wax—to Bleach.—Bees-wax is obtained by washing and melting. The comb is yellow. Wax is freed from its impurities, and bleached by melting it with hot water or steam, in a tinned copper or wooden vessel, letting it settle, running it off into an .oblong trough with a line of holes in its bottom, so as to distribute it upon horizontal wooden cylinders made to revolve half immersed in cold water, and then exposing the thin ribbons or films thus obtained to the blanching action of air, light, and moisture. For this purpose the ribbons are laid upon long webs of canvas stretched horizontally between standards, two feet above the surface of a sheltered field, having a free exposure to the sunbeams. Here they are frequently turned over, then covered by nets to prevent their being blown away by winds, and watered from time to time, like linen upon the grass field in the old method of bleaching. Whenever the color of the wax seems stationary, it is collected, re-melted, and thrown again into ribbons upon the wet cylinder, in order to expose new surfaces to the bleaching operation. By several repetitions of these processes, if the weather proves favorable, the wax becomes quite white.

Zinc, To Pulverize.—Zinc, though a tough metal at ordinary temperatures, is exceedingly brittle when heated to nearly its melting point. To reduce it to powder, therefore, the best plan is to pour melted zinc into a dry and warm cast-iron mortar, and as soon as it shows signs of solidifying pound it with the pestle. In this way it may be reduced to a very fine powder.

OF

Books and Periodicals

PUBLISHED AND FOR SALE BY

THE INDUSTRIAL PUBLICATION COMPANY,

176 Broadway, New York.

☞ *Any of these Books may be obtained from any Bookseller or Newsdealer, or will be sent Free by mail to any part of the United States or Canada ON RECEIPT OF PRICE.*

The Amateur's Handbook of Practical Information,

For the Workshop and the Laboratory.   Second Edition.
Greatly Enlarged.   Neatly Bound   -   15 cents.

This is a handy little book, containing just the information needed by Amateurs in the Workshop and Laboratory.   Directions for making Alloys, Fusible Metals, Cements, Glues, etc.; and for Soldering, Brazing, Lacquering, Bronzing, Staining and Polishing Wood, Tempering Tools, Cutting and Working Glass, Varnishing, Silvering, Gilding, Preparing Skins, etc., etc.

The New Edition contains extended directions for preparing Polishing Powders, Freezing Mixtures, Colored Lights for tableaux, Solutions for rendering ladies' dresses incombustible, etc.   There has also been added a very large number of new and valuable receipts.

Rhymes of Science: Wise and Otherwise.

By O. W. Holmes, Bret Hart, Ingoldsby, Prof. Forbes, Prof. J. W. McQ. Rankine, Hon. R. W. Raymond, and others.
With Illustrations.   Cloth, Gilt Title.   -   50 cents.

Instruction in the Art of Wood Engraving.

A Manual of Instruction in the Art of Wood Engraving; with a Description of the Necessary Tools and Apparatus, and Concise Directions for their Use; Explanation of the Terms Used, and the Methods Employed for Producing the Various Classes of Wood Engravings. By S. E. Fuller.

Fully illustrated with Engravings by the author, separate sheets of engravings for transfer and practice being added.

New Edition, Neatly Bound. - - 30 cents.

What to Do in Case of Accident.

What to Do and How to Do It in Case of Accident. A Book for Everybody. 12mo., Cloth, Gilt Title. 50 cents.

This is one of the most useful books ever published. It tells exactly what to do in case of accidents, such as Severe Cuts, Sprains, Dislocations, Broken Bones, Burns with Fire, Scalds, Burns with Corrosive Chemicals, Sunstroke, Suffocation by Foul Air, Hanging, Drowning, Frost-Bite, Fainting, Stings, Bites, Starvation, Lightning, Poisons, Accidents from Machinery, and from the Falling of Scaffolding, Gunshot Wounds, etc., etc. It ought to be in every house, for young and old are liable to accident, and the directions given in this book might be the means of saving many a valuable life.

BOUND VOLUMES OF

The Technologist, or Industrial Monthly.

The eight volumes of THE TECHNOLOGIST, OR INDUSTRIAL MONTHLY, which have been issued, form a Mechanical and Architectural Encyclopædia of great value; and, when properly bound, they form a most important addition to any library. The splendid full-page engravings, printed on tinted paper, in the highest style of the art, are universally conceded to be the finest architectural and mechanical engravings ever published in this country. We have on hand a few complete sets, which we offer for $16.00, handsomely and uniformly bound in cloth.

We have also a few extra sets of Vols. III to VIII inclusive. These six volumes we offer for $8.00 bound in cloth. As there are but a very few sets remaining, those who desire to secure them should order the Wing. With Useful Hints concerning all that relates to Guns and Shooting, and particularly in regard to the art of Loading so as to Kill. To which has been added several Valuable and hitherto Secret Recipes, of Great Practical Importance to the Sportsman. By an Old Gamekeeper.

12mo., Cloth, Gilt Title. - - - 75 cents.

The Pistol as a Weapon of Defence,

In the House and on the Road.

12mo., Cloth. - - - - - 50 cents.

This work aims to instruct the peaceable and law-abiding citizens in the best means of protecting themselves from the attacks of the brutal and the lawless, and is the only practical book published on this subject. Its contents are as follows: The Pistol as a Weapon of Defence.—The Carrying of Fire-Arms.—Different kinds of Pistols in Market; How to Choose a Pistol.—Ammunition, different kinds; Powder, Caps, Bullets, Copper Cartridges, etc.—Best form of Bullet.—How to Load.—Best Charge for Pistols.—How to regulate the Charge.—Care of the Pistol; how to Clean it.—How to Handle and Carry the Pistol.—How to Learn to Shoot.—Practical use of the Pistol; how to Protect yourself and how to Disable your antagonist.

Lightning Rods.

Plain Directions for the Construction and Erection of Lightning Rods. By John Phin, C. E., editor of "The Young Scientist," author of "Chemical History of the Six Days of the Creation," etc. Second Edition. Enlarged and Fully Illustrated.

12mo., Cloth, Gilt Title. - - .. 50 cents.

This is a simple and practical little work, intended to convey just such information as will enable every property owner to decide whether or not his buildings are thoroughly protected. It is not written in the interest of any patent or particular article of manufacture, and by following its directions, any ordinarily skilful mechanic can put up a rod that will afford perfect protection, and that will not infringe any patent. Every owner of a house or barn ought to procure a copy.

POPULAR SCIENCE.

PROSPECTUS.

The object of the JOURNAL OF MICROSCOPY is to diffuse a knowledge of the best methods of using the Microscope; of all valuable improvements in the instrument and its accessories; of all new methods of microscopical investigation, and of the most recent results of microscopical research. The JOURNAL does not address itself to those who have long pursued certain special lines of research, and whose wants can be supplied only by elaborate papers, which, from their thoroughness, are entitled to be called monographs rather than mere articles. It is intended rather to meet the wants of those who use the microscope for purposes of general study, medical work, class insruction, and even amusement, and who desire, in addition to the information afforded by text-books, such a knowledge of what others are doing as can be derived only from a periodical. With this object in view, therefore, the publishers propose to make the JOURNAL so simple, practical and trustworthy, that it will prove to the advantage of every one who uses the microscope at all to take it.

ILLUSTRATIONS.—The JOURNAL will be freely illustrated by engravings representing either objects of natural history or apparatus connected with the microscope.

TRANSACTIONS OF SOCIETIES.—THE AMERICAN JOURNAL OF MICROSCOPY is not the organ of any Society, but it gives the proceedings of all Societies whose officers send us a report. As the JOURNAL is devoted *wholly* to Microscopy, and is in good form and size for binding, no better medium can be had for preserving the scientific records of any society. Matters of mere business routine we are frequently obliged to omit for want of room.

EXCHANGES.—An important feature of the JOURNAL is the exchange column, by means of which workers in different parts of the country are enabled, without expense, except for postage, to exchange slides and materials with each other.

TERMS.

During the first two years of its existence, the subscription to the AMERICAN JOURNAL OF MICROSCOPY was only fifty cents per year, but at the request of more than two-thirds of the subscribers, the size of the JOURNAL has been doubled, and the price raised to

ONE DOLLAR PER YEAR.

Four copies for three dollars. Those who wish to economize in the direction of periodicals, would do well to examine our clubbing list.

FOREIGN SUBSCRIBERS.—The JOURNAL will be sent, postage paid, to any country in the Postal Union for $1.24, or 6 shillings sterling per year. English postage stamps, American currency or American postage stamps taken in payment. In return for a postal order or draft for £1 5s., five copies of the JOURNAL will be furnished and mailed to different addresses. Make all drafts and postal orders payable to John Phin.

BACK VOLUMES.—We have on hand a few copies of Vols. I and II, bound in handsome cloth cases, which we offer for $1 25 each. Vols. I and II, bound, and the numbers of Vol. III, as issued, we offer for $2.50. We can no longer supply complete sets of 1876–7 in sheets. To those who wish to examine the journal, we will send ten odd numbers for 25 cents.

Advertisements.

The JOURNAL OF MICROSCOPY, from its very nature, is a visitor to the very best families, and its value as an advertising medium has therefore proved to be much above that of average periodicals. A few select advertisements will be inserted at the rate of 30 cents per line, nonpariel measure, of which twelve lines make an inch. Address

AMERICAN JOURNAL OF MICROSCOPY,
P. O. Box 4875, New York.

HOW TO USE THE MICROSCOPE.

A Simple and Practical Book, intended for beginners.

By JOHN PHIN,

Editor of "The American Journal of Microscopy."

Second Edition. Greatly Enlarged, with 50 illustrations in the text, and 4 full-page engravings printed on heavy tint paper.

CONTENTS:

WHAT A MICROSCOPE IS.—Different Kinds of Microscopes.—Simple Microscopes.—Hand Magnifiers.—The Coddington Lens.—The Stanhope Lens.—Raspail's Microscope.—The Excelsior Microscope.—Twenty-five cent Microscopes and how to make them.—Penny Microscopes.

COMPOUND MICROSCOPES.—Different kinds of Objectives.—Non-Achromatic Objectives.—French Achromatic Objectives—Objectives of the English Form.—Immersion Objectives—Focal Lengths corresponding to the numbers employed by Nachet, Hartnack and Gundlach.

HOW TO CHOOSE A MICROSCOPE.—Microscopes for Special Purposes.—Magnifying Power required for different purposes.—How to judge of the quality of the different parts of the Microscope.

ACCESSORY APPARATUS.—Stage Forceps, Animalcule Cage, etc.

ILLUMINATION.—Sun Light.—Artificial Light.—Bulls-Eye Condenser.—Side Reflector.—The Lieberkuhn.—Axial Light.—Oblique Light.—Direct Light.

HOW TO USE THE MICROSCOPE.—How to Care for the Microscope.

HOW TO COLLECT OBJECTS.—Where to find Objects.—What to Look for.—How to Capture Them.—Nets.—Bottle-Holders.—Spoons.—New Form of Collecting Bottle.—Aquaria for Microscopic Objects.—Dipping Tubes.

THE PREPARATION AND EXAMINATION OF OBJECTS.—Cutting Thin Sections of Soft Substances.—Sections of Wood and Bone.—Improved Section Cutter.—Sections of Rock.—Knives.—Scissors.—Needles.—Dissecting Pans and Dishes.—Dissecting - Microscopes.—Separation of Deposits from Liquids.—Preparing whole Insects.—Feet, Eyes, Tongues, Wings, etc., of Insects.—Use of Chemical Tests.—Liquids for Moistening Objects.—Refractive Power of Liquids.—Covers for Keeping out Dust.—Errors in Microscopical Observations.

PRESERVATION OF OBJECTS.—General Principles.—Recipes for Preservative Fluids.—General Rules for Applying them.

MOUNTING OBJECTS.—Apparatus and Materials for: Slides, Covers, Cells, Turn-Table, Cards for Making Cells, Hot-Plate, Lamps, Retort Stand, Slide-Holder, Mounting Needles, Cover Forceps, Simple Form of Spring Clip, Centering Cards, Gold Size, Black Japan, Brunswick Black, Shellac, Bell's Cement, Sealing Wax Varnish, Colored Shellac, Damar Cement, Marine Glue, Liquid Glue, Dextrine.—Mounting Transparent Objects Dry.—Mounting in[sects.—How] ng of Whole Insects.—How que Objects.

FINISHING

May be obta r will be sent by

THE INDUSTRIAL PUBLICATION COMPANY

Lightning Source UK Ltd.
Milton Keynes UK
UKHW02f2039170418
321226UK00018B/322/P